FOUR PLAYS

1996

FOUR PLAYS

Compiled and Introduced by
Zakes Mda

Published by
Vivlia Publishers & Booksellers (Pty) Ltd
PO Box 1040
FLORIDA HILLS
1716

Telephone: National (011) 472-3912
             International +27 11 472-3912
Fax: (011) 472-4904

First edition, first impression 1996

ISBN 1-86867-058-9

Set by Graphco Processing, Cape Town

Printed and bound by CTP Books

Cover designed by Graphco Processing

CONTENTS

1. Introduction – An Overview of Theatre   vi
   in South Africa

2. So What's New By Fatima Dike   1

3. Umongikazi/The Nurse By Maishe Maponya   49

4. The Nun's Romantic Story By Zakes Mda   77

5. Member of Society By Makwedini Mtsaka   124

INTRODUCTION: An Overview of Theatre in South Africa

Art and Politics

When Albie Sachs (1990) made his controversial proposition that ANC members should be banned for five years from saying that culture is a weapon of struggle, he provoked a barrage of responses in the print media, and in seminars and conferences. This proposition, which stimulated so much unprecedented debate, was initially made by him in a paper titled "Preparing Ourselves for Freedom" which he presented at an inhouse seminar on culture organized by the ANC in Lusaka in 1989. It reached South Africa through the pages of **The Weekly Mail.** His major concern was that the work of the artist had deteriorated to the levels of sloganeering, masquerading as art. He wrote

> *Instead of getting real criticism, we get solidarity criticism. Our artists are not pushed to improve the quality of their work, it is enough that it is politically correct. The more fists, and spears, and guns, the better. The range of themes is narrowed down so much that all that is funny or curious or genuinely tragic in the world is extruded. (p20)*

There were three strands that one could clearly observe in the responses that came, mostly from the artists themselves — or from cultural workers, as some artists prefer to be called — and from the critics. The first one, which articulated itself through the voices of such critics as Meintjies (1990) was in agreement with Sachs. Indeed, the voice said, sloganeering was a barrier to depth and genuine expression. Some other writers were cited, such as novelist Nadine Gordimer, Congress of South African Writers president Njabulo Ndebele and poet Chris van Wyk, who had on earlier occasions, long before Sachs' controversial paper, been crusading for an art that went beyond the knee-jerk responses to the hurt caused by apartheid. The voice went further to state that on the theatre front practitioners such as actor/director John Kani, worker-culture programmes director Ari Sitas, and arts editor Tyrone August, had long been complaining about the clichés and hackneyed approaches found in much of "protest" drama. Theatre practitioners who produced to a set formula were slammed for a lack of depth, since their work was "abounding in stereotypes, aimed more at overseas audiences than at the community at home." (p34) A careful rider was added though that art could not "absolve itself from facing the ugly social realities of South Africa today." (p31)

The second strand came from the militant cultural worker who insists that culture is a weapon of struggle, and as such it should be used. This artist does not apologize for sloganeering, for it is through slogans that the audiences are mobilized and rallied around a particular cause. The artist here does not pretend to be interested in creating works that will be of lasting value. He or she creates for the occasion, and the work may or may not live beyond the occasion. Indeed some writers got involved in a medium like theatre because they had a political agenda, and thought that theatre would be most effective in expressing their political ideas. We shall come back to this perspective when we examine the various categories of theatre that exist in South Africa.

The third strand was that of the "liberal" artist and critic, who read in Sachs' propositions a long-awaited admission from the saner ranks of the liberation movement that it had been detrimental to link art with politics. This was a position that asserted the autonomy and the permanence of the work of art, and the right of the artist as an individual to pursue his or her vision of the beautiful and the excellent without reference to ulterior ends. (Brink: 1991:1) This was an art for art's sake position, for it was emphatic in its assertion that the South African artist must create work that is not expected to, and indeed should not, be put to any practical use nor fulfil any ulterior function. Ahmed (1990) commented on this position and expressed the concerns of those who operated within cultural structures that espoused a different view, when he wrote

> Liberals vociferously reaffirm their position — that they were right all along and that art must be divorced from politics. The paper [Sachs'] has caused some consternation within the mass based progressive movement, where cultural workers (as Ari Sitas puts it) are worried that their work has been banal or even devoid of content. (p121)

It is clear that Sachs' concern in his original proposition was on quality, or lack of it, in the work of the constituency he was addressing. He had no intention of taking the "aesthetic position" in what Brink (1991,1) calls "the immemorial debate between the aesthetic and the political". In an interview with a journal of South African cultural workers published in London Sachs says that he has been "praised for things I didn't say. I certainly don't believe you can ever separate art from politics, most definitely not in South Africa." (Langa 1990, 30)

The separation of art, and specifically of theatre, from politics is an illusive notion; and when one examines the different genres of theatre that exist in South Africa, it certainly has not been a factor in the production and enjoyment of the art in this country. It is generally taken for granted that the creator of theatre selects her or his material from life, and from his or her society. And of course South Africa was a society characterized by racial segregation, political oppression, and economic exploitation. South African theatre could never be abstracted from that particular context. The writer in South Africa, particularly the black writer, was not, to use Brink's (1991, 17) words, "writing about 'something out there' when he/she draws politics into the text: it is part and parcel of the most intimate experience of his/her daily life". Even an author like Athol Fugard, who is of a liberal tradition, and has on previous occasions incurred the wrath of the mass based cultural movement when he stood as a lone voice that opposed the cultural boycott of South Africa, has unequivocally supported this view. In his graduation address on the receipt of an honorary degree at the University of the Witwatersrand he said that he was often inclined to forget just how politicized the South African environment was compared with most other "Western societies". He went further to say

> When I am asked, for example, outside South Africa, the relationship between politics and my play writing, I answer with total honesty that I don't really give the matter any thought. I point out that, as far as I am concerned, in the South African context the two are inseparable. I think of myself essentially as a story-teller, and as such, the notion that there could be such a thing as an apolitical South African story is a contradiction in terms. (Fugard 1992, 66)

I have said that art cannot be abstracted from its particular context, but the South African context is richer and more varied than the theatre has attempted to depict. For a long time now, a dominant trend in the types of theatre that exist in South Africa has been based on a unidimensional and prevaricated depiction of the South African reality. For example, the playwright wrote about those men who went to jail, and examined their sufferings and — in a later phase of his writing — their resistance. He told the story of those who laboured in the belly of the earth to make white South Africa rich. He clearly depicted their condition, their trials, their struggles, and in some cases their defiance and determination to change their situation. But he forgot to tell the story of those who did not follow them to jail or to the mines — the women and children who stayed at home and struggled to make the stubborn and barren soil yield.

The South Africa of his theatre was basically an urban and a male one. The observation that Ndebele (1984) made on South African literature in general, that the city had a tyrannical hold on the imagination of the average African writer, applied to theatre as well. Peasants and other rural dwellers were ignored as subjects of artistic attention. Once in awhile, on very rare occasions, there would be a bright spark that would illuminate other aspects of the people's life, such as Gcina Mhlophe's (1988) **Have You Seen Zandile?**, an auto-biographical two-hander that examined the life of a young woman growing up in rural South Africa. Other exceptions were **You Strike the Woman, You Strike the Rock** which examined the role that women played in the South African liberation struggle, and **Imfuduso**, which was on the question of forced removals, in this case at Crossroads in Cape Town. It is significant that these plays were either wholly created (written, directed, and performed) by women, as is the case with Mhlophe's play, or women played a major role in creating them. **Imfuduso** was of special significance in that it was performed by the Crossroads women themselves, and depicted their own struggles in resisting forced removals. Generally the South African theatre practitioner shied away from depicting social and class conflicts among the oppressed themselves, and rarely did we see the family — even that one which has been broken down by the laws of apartheid — as a subject for his theatre.

It will be noted that I do not mention such plays as **Ipi-tombi** or **Kwa-Zulu** which were set or partially set in the rural areas. These plays, conceived and produced by white entre-preneurs, never created or recreated any aspect of the South African reality, but were rooted in their own fantastical world. They were abortive attempts to glorify the government's Bantustan policies. As a result they never gained any popularity in South Africa, except with the white middle class and overseas tourists. One critic (Horn 1986, 213) referred to this as the Theatre of Exploitation, and has described it thus

> *A great emphasis was on spectacle and little on plot and character development; the values and mores of traditional*

African societies, often tempered by Christianity, are extolled, the material environments of such societies romanticized, and the rural setting demonstrated to be more congenial for blacks than that of the towns and cities.

This was a theatre of titillation, of the swinging pelvis and the tantalizing naked breast. It was a theatre of the perpetually happy native who sang and danced at the slightest provocation, particularly when he or she was in her or his natural idyllic rural environment. Love bloomed in these villages, birds sang, and maidens served their menfolk calabashes of beer against the background of bucolic sunsets and exotic lullabies. Rural poverty, unemployment, and sickness, did not exist. The obvious conclusion that one was expected to draw was that apartheid or 'separate development' with its Bantustan relocation policies was reasonable, humane and historically legitimate.

Alternative Theatre and Other Labels

South African theatre is not a homogenous monolith. It has trends and distinct categories whose social function is varied. What has been seen outside South Africa, touring European and American venues, represents only one or two categories of what makes South African theatre. Some scholars have referred to the theatre that I will discuss in this Introduction as "alternative theatre".

It is a theatre, they say, which is revolutionary in nature, and challenges the established "white, heterosexual, culturally exclusive norms and values" (Angove 1992, 40). What this label implies is that in South Africa there are established theatrical traditions to which this theatre has emerged as an alternative. But we are not told what these established and acknowledged traditions are.

There is an English South African theatre which has been, as Angove (1992, 41) points out, "characterized by a colonial mentality, still searching for and finding theatrical roots 'home' in England"; and a traditional Afrikaans theatre which has been rooted in the movement whose goal was to establish a body of Afrikaans literature that would enhance the Afrikaner identity. Both these two theatres were established and acknowledged in their respective communities. But this was by no means the theatre of the majority of the South African population. I certainly do not consider Gibson Kente's musical theatre, which for decades has enjoyed popular following throughout South Africa, and has influenced at least two generations of theatre practitioners in this country, or Athol Fugard's erudite theatre which also had its large following among the black intelligentsia and liberal white middle classes, as alternative to any other form of theatre that exists in South Africa today. The same applies to the pan-African theatre of Matsemela Manaka, the harrowing comedies and tragi-comedies of Paul Slabolepszy, the musicals of Mbongeni Ngema, the workshopped plays of Barney Simon, the political satires of Pieter-Dirk Uys, the work of the 'young angry Afrikaners' such as Deon Opperman, and the plays of Ronnie Govender that tell the story of the "Indian" people of South Africa. The work of all these playwrights and directors is not alternative, but representative of the different categories of the mainstream South African theatre.

The first category of South African theatre that I must briefly discuss is that of the indigenous modes of performance that are precolonial, but extant particularly in the rural areas of South Africa. These include praise performance poetry known as **dithoko** in Sesotho or **izibongo** in Zulu. It also includes dance performance modes such as **dipina tsa mokopu** in Sesotho which are performed at harvest time, and reflect the world in which girls and young women live, and the social relations in the village. Each ethnic group in South Africa has its own performance modes ranging from para-theatrical religious ritual to folk narratives that are performed by a single actor who assumes the roles of all the different characters in the play: the Zulu **inganekwane**, the Xhosa

intsomi, and the Sotho **tshomo.** All these modes have highly developed dramatic elements, and are gaining particular significance with the new popular theatre movement that is emerging in the country.

One major category of South African theatre that has been dominant for three decades, and has been popular throughout the country, is referred to by critics as Township Musical Theatre. It is called that because it is rooted in the townships. It emanated from them, and rarely emerged from township venues. The major practitioner in the genre was Gibson Kente who, since 1960, created plays that were performed by his travelling company even in the smallest towns of South Africa and neighbouring states such as Lesotho and Botswana. This theatre was characterized by the extensive use of music and dance. Kente is highly proficient in musical composition and in choreography. He is also credited with the invention of a peculiar style of acting which is full of energy and is spectacularly over-theatrical. It is a style characterized by bulging eyes, wide open mouths, heavily punctuated dialogue, and exaggerated movements. Kente has been so much of a major force in South African theatre that many playwrights, actors and directors, working in the theatre in South Africa today have at one stage worked under him. His method of acting has therefore diffused itself even in other categories of theatre that are not Township Musical Theatre. One critic wrote

> *The approach worked well in the past when it had been creatively adapted for theatre and used in such plays as* **Sarafina, Asinamali** *and to an extent* **Bopha**. *Percy Mtwa, Mbongeni Ngema and even pop singer Brenda Fassie, are all referred to as "Gibson [Kente's] Products". (Leshoai 1989, 6)*

Township Musical Theatre was very formulaic, and like the European and American melodrama of the 19th century it had its stock characters. In every play the audience would expect to see a dimwitted policeman, often brutal, a priest, a comical school teacher, a shebeen queen, a township gossip who is also a comic relief character, a diviner, a streetwise fast talking hoodlum, and a beautiful 'sexy' girl. The plot would involve a church service usually of the African independent churches known as Zionist, a wedding, a jail scene, and a funeral. There would be plenty of slapstick humour, and of weeping. The story would not be overtly political, except in rare cases such as in Kente's **Too Late, How Long,** and **I Believe**. Township Musical Theatre dealt with the sensational side of life: prostitution, adultery, rape, and divorce. These themes were examined in a simplistic manner, which disregarded causality, and served on the whole to endorse and promote official values. Horn (1984) has this to say about this theatre

> *The narrowed and absolutist melodramatic vision also characterizes the plays of Gibson Kente, South Africa's most prominent black playwright-producer and one of the progenitors of the modern black urban theatre. In more than a score of plays for stage and television, Kente's argument has remained essentially the same: work within the system, get educated, reject temptation, maintain family cohesion, accumulate wealth through personal industry and, perhaps, encourage orderly reform — but never the radical revision of the existing scheme of things.*

This critic has referred to this as the Theatre of Acceptance and Lament. It reached its peak of popularity throughout the 1970s, with long running productions by such playwrights as Sam Mhangwane **(Unfaithful Woman, Ma-in-Law)** and Boikie Mohlamme **(Mahlomola)** touring the townships throughout Southern Africa. Today the popularity of Township Musical Theatre has tremendously waned, although its impact continues to be strong in the current trends.

Another category of South African theatre has been referred to, for want of a better name, as Town Theatre. It is called that because it is performed in purpose-built city venues, and rarely does it go to the townships. This is the kind of theatre whose main focus is on the production of a creative product, rather than on consumption. It is therefore an erudite theatre that employs theatrical codes that need a more intellectual interpretation than does Township Musical Theatre. Town Theatre is created by both black and white intermediate classes, whereas Township Musical Theatre is created solely by black practitioners who run commercial theatre companies. Town Theatre is based on traditional Western models in form, or on more experimental international modes, although the content is South Africa. Township Musical Theatre on the other hand is highly syncretic, using both popular indigenous African modes and Western ones. In most cases Town Theatre will deal with political themes, and when it does it becomes a "protest theatre".

It is important to note how the label "protest theatre" is used here. There has been a tendency in the South African media to refer to any play that treats political themes as "protest". Not all political theatre is protest theatre. Least of all, agitprop cannot be protest. That would be a contradiction in terms. Protest theatre makes a statement of disapproval or disagreement, but does not go beyond that. It addresses itself to the oppressor, with the view of appealing to his conscience. It is a theatre of complaint, or sometimes even of weeping. It is variously a theatre of self-pity, of moralizing, of mourning, and of hopelessness. It never offers any solution beyond the depiction of the sad situation in which the people find themselves.

An example of this category can be found in a number of Athol Fugard's plays, particularly his earlier works. His plays have depicted various aspects of segregation in South Africa, such as the Immorality Act in **Statements**, racial classification in **The Blood Knot**, and the Group Areas Act in **Boesman and Lena**. These plays clearly protest against racial segregation by depicting its inhuman nature. But these works have some prevarications in their depiction of the South African reality. The oppressed suffer in silence, and are not involved in any struggle against the oppression. Instead they are endowed with endless reservoirs of stoic endurance. The spirit of defiance that exists in the real life situation is non-existent in these works. When one has seen a play like **Boesman and Lena**, and one is not at all familiar with the situation in South Africa, and with the fact that people in South Africa have struggled and fought against oppression in different ways, one is left with the impression that the blacks really deserved to be oppressed, for they let oppression happen to them.

Fugard, like Kente, has had a big impact on South African theatre. His theatre, and that of a number of Town Theatre practitioners such as Barney Simon, has been seen a great deal in American and European venues. Inside South Africa a number of practitioners of all races were influenced by Fugard, and also by Simon.

Some theatre practitioners in South Africa went beyond protest, a position which began with the advent of the Black Consciousness movement in the 1970s. The case against protest theatre was that by its nature it attempted to reveal the blacks to the whites, and placed the onus on the blacks to prove their humanity. The theatre practitioner was no longer interested in creating a theatre of complaint. This position gained momentum in the early 1980s. It is during this period that the Theatre of Resistance which was quite distinct from the protest of Town Theater gained a mass following, and became the main genre with practitioners from all the ideological leanings in the South African liberation politics spectrum.

Whereas protest theatre addressed itself to the oppressor, this new theatre addressed itself directly to the oppressed with the overt aim of rallying or of mobilizing the oppressed to explore ways and means of fighting against the oppression. It was agitprop, for it attempted to propagate a message, and agitate for action on the part of the oppressed to change their situation. It was a theatre which at its best, served as a vehicle for sharing perceptions and insights among the oppressed themselves, and more importantly which attempted to alter perception. At its worst it became a litany of slogans that denounced the oppressor, and extolled the virtues and prowess of the leaders of the liberation struggle.

Matsemela Manaka was one of the more creative practitioners of Theatre of Resistance. His play, **Egoli** (1979), was well-received when it opened at the People's Space Theatre in Cape Town under the directorship of Rob Amato. The play is set in the hostel of a male workers' compound at a gold mine. It centres around the relationship between, and the experiences of, two migrant workers. It has sharp, short scenes, each, according to Larlham (1985, 86), "a heightened poetic image of the workers' experience, past and present." Larlham goes further to say

> These sequences, metaphors for the plight of the Black man, contain little realistic dialogue. The violent ritual removal of the shackles, for example, is accompanied by a chant, "people share Egoli ["city of gold" (Johannesburg)], people die Egoli, "and a song "How we fight for my freedom." Once they are freed, Hamilton [one of the characters] makes an invocation for positive action: "now that you are free do not wait for life to happen to you — make it happen." This is followed by a song of hope. (p87)

The setting of **Egoli** is stark, and the play depends very much on dream sequences, role-play, and flashbacks. It is highly stylized rather than naturalistic, and sets and props are sparsely used. It is a theatre that depends more on human resources rather than on the paraphernalia of the stage. This became the common method of staging with all the Theatre of Resistance that followed. Of course the stark and sparse stage was not Manaka's invention. Fugard used it. And so did Jerzy Grotowski in Europe. Another example of this genre is **Asinamali** by Mbongeni Ngema.

Whereas Township Musical Theatre was confined to the

townships and Town Theatre kept itself in the purpose-built city venues, Theatre of Resistance — which was called the Theatre of Criticism and Confrontation by Horn (1986, 213) — crossed barriers, and was seen at weddings and funerals, at political rallies, in church and school halls in the townships, and in city venues such as the Market Theatre. It even took over from Town Theatre as South Africa's main theatre export.

By the late 1980s Theatre of Resistance had become the dominant genre in South Africa, and very little was being heard of Township Musical Theatre. A great number of the practitioners who used to produce Township Musical Theatre adopted Theatre of Resistance. It became a powerful political weapon which was promoted by the mass based political movement that was active inside the country at the time. As Fugard (1992, 72) says, "The drama in the streets [was] being so immediately reflected by the drama on the stage." However the unfortunate development at this time was that the "resistance" in these plays was only in content, and not in function. With the opening of city venues to all races, there was a movement of theatre production away from the people in the township. In the heyday of Township Musical Theatre people in the townships had access to theatre, for it was performed in their midst in township venues. It was not unusual for a labourer who had been digging trenches on the road all day, to go and see a Kente play at Diepkloof Hall in the evening. Theatre was not an elitist activity as it has become in the Western world. The irony of it all was that the more the theatre became radical in South Africa, the more it became revolutionary in content, the more it moved away from the people. By 1990 almost all relevant theatre of the Theatre of Resistance category was performed only in city venues, and the audiences were white liberals and sprinklings of members of the black middle class who could afford to drive to these expensive venues. There were a few groups that would begin their work in the townships. But even these aspired to be in the city venues, and would indeed end up there when they got the necessary recognition from the white managed theatre establishments. The establishment would then reshape these productions, and add the essential slickness, in readiness for the export market. Those members of the working class who used to enjoy theatre were now deprived of it. They could not afford to travel to the city in the evenings to see a play. Besides transport problems, ticket prices were prohibitive. Politically committed groups like the Cape Flat Players, however, before they took their Theatre of Resistance plays to the Baxter Theatre in Cape Town, they would tour some of the most marginalized areas in the Western Cape. Thamm (1989, 25) reports that over the years the group's productions, which included **Inkululeko Ngoku-Freedom Now!, Senzenina?, Aluta Continua, Dit Sal Die Blerrie Dag Wees,** and **What About De Lo**, were seen by over 600 000 people from the remotest villages to major city centres. The Cape Flat Players were an exception rather than the rule.

A further irony was that the opening of city venues to all races took the theatre away from the people. In the heyday of apartheid, when these city venues were closed to black people, the theatre was with the people in the townships. Today it is the ambition of most playwrights to have a play at the Market Theatre, and then of course in Europe and America. Writers now write purely for export, and design their plays in a manner which they think will be acceptable to overseas audiences. A critic wrote of one of such plays

> *This brings one to the core of the problem in **Sarafina** [by Mbongeni Ngema]. With its bowler hats and designer glamour, it is earmarked: export. While extremely informative to Broadway audiences, to local audiences it states the familiar and obvious, giving it a simplistic and superficial quality that demeans the events being dealt with. (Le Roux 1989)*

Although Ngema's work played to full houses at the Market Theatre (I counted an audience that was 96% white at one performance, and this was quite normal for this venue even for those plays that are regarded as "black"), the South African critics have not been kind to him. Barry Ronge (1990, 15) of the **Sunday Times** says Ngema's work, with the single exception of **Asinamali**, is trite. He says a play like **Township Fever**, for instance, lacks dramatic substance, effective characterization, intellectual complexity, and subtle acting: "It is so naively poor, yet so richly opportunistic that it simply outraged me." Another critic, Minervini (1990, 8) says the play is likely to engender more critical enthusiasm on Broadway than in Johannesburg. Ngema, she says, uses images that have long lost their theatrical currency in South Africa because the toyi-toyi, the raised fist and "amandla!" will still thrill a New York audience. If Ronge and Minervini were representative of the white liberal press, the black press was even more scathing. Nyantsumba (1991, 68) writes that commercialization and commercialism have reduced black South African theatre to

> a predictable and woefully disappointing parochial art. We are fast reaching a stage where there is no art in local black theatre, but an assemblage of familiar anti-apartheid signs, images and slogans which appeal only to one's emotions. These unfortunately are plays that go on to win award after award in Europe and the US, and all because they predictably deliver that anti-apartheid message people overseas yearn to hear.

This critic goes further to say that **Sarafina** was a commercial success but certainly not an artistic success: the play was well-directed and meticulously choreographed, but lacked both plot and main theme.

One very significant factor about the work of Mbongeni Ngema is that it has successfully combined the elements of Township Musical Theatre with those of Theatre of Resistance. He considers his work as falling into a new category which he calls Theatre of Liberation. He says that Theatre of Liberation is a more useful and inspirational alternative to protest theatre. Such theatre, he says, strives to free the audience from the psychological legacy of oppression; and the success of **Sarafina** was due to its accent on liberation (Wren 1990, 28). Alas, the audiences that were liberated from the "psychological legacy of oppression" were not those from the townships and rural areas who form the vast majority of the oppressed in South Africa, for they never saw the play.

I have come across the question from overseas audiences, "If the South African regime was so oppressive, how come these plays were allowed to go on?" The answer, of course, is that although these plays were militant in content, they were quite harmless to the regime since they were performed at venues whose majority patronage was that of white liberals ("preaching to the converted" the saying went in South Africa). They did not reach the real people who were capable of taking revolutionary action after being rallied and mobilized by the works. Theatre practitioners who operated at grassroots level were always harassed by the state, and even arrested. For quite some time the state machinery of censorship was erratic and bungling. But even the censor was smart enough to realise that the fact that these works were confined to special venues in the city, and then were exported abroad, they could actually do more good for the South African government than harm. For instance, they created a false illusion of a democratic environment, with healthy dosages of freedom of expression, that supposedly existed in South Africa, where the government could be criticized so vehemently, yet the works continued to be staged. Whereas the government did not hesitate to take immediate and overt action against grassroot theatrical operations, covert action was taken against targeted performers even in city venues. For instance Potgieter (1992, X5) of the **Sunday Times** uncovered a unit run jointly by the South African Defence Force and the Johannesburg City Council. Among its projects was to assault actors Andre-Jacques van der Merwe and Andre Lombard who were taking part in an anti-war play, **Somewhere on the Border**. All these plans were made at the SADF headquarters in Pretoria, at the time when the "anti-conscription fever" was mounting. The objective was to stop the production. This was the same covert unit which disrupted and teargassed a concert by singer Jennifer Fergusson at the Market Theatre.

The plays in this Collection

It is not the intention of this Introduction to present a detailed discussion of the plays in this collection. I leave it to the reader, the teacher and the student, to make their own critical evaluation of the plays, and to place them in their proper context.

The four plays are by authors who have made their mark in the South African theatre scene for more than two decades. Their previous work is represented in the various categories discussed in this Introduction.

Three of the plays represent a new post-apartheid theatre that is gradually emerging. **Member of Society** was performed to great acclaim in the cities of the Eastern Cape in 1994. It is an allegory that addresses pertinent issues in today's South Africa: liberation, justice, forgiveness and reconciliation. It asserts that we have a lot to learn from African values, and espouses a humanistic philosophy known as ubuntu — "I am because we are." It certainly probes the creation of a new South African society.

Watson (1994) wrote: "Forgiving and forgetting is always easier said than done and when that burden is placed on a whole society, the task is even harder. That is the theme of this play and the problems and possible solutions facing the people around us are explored and dealt with."

So What's New, on the other hand, took both Cape Town and Johannesburg by storm when it was performed in those cities in 1991. It was a new kind of black South African theatre, a domestic comedy that was not overtly political. Indeed politics features only as a backdrop to the social inter-action of the characters. The play explores the struggle and resilience of three township women who have to make their living legally and illegally as the system allows. One runs a shebeen, another sells real estate, and yet another one survives on peddling drugs. They escape in television soap operas, and vicariously live their risky lives through the exaggerated lives of soap opera characters. The play also explores the domestic lives of the youth who are committed to changing their society in times of great violence.

The play is an indictment of our times, where the lives of ordinary citizens are sullied in a quagmire of crime and violence. It is also an indictment of the society which allows women like Thandi to resort to drug smuggling in order to survive. Here crime is rewarded, for she is finally able to buy her own house. The author is able to explore these lives without passing judgement on any of her characters, and without preaching.

The Nun's Romantic Story takes a different direction from the previous two plays. It is not set in South Africa, but in an unspecified "Third World" country. In fact, the play was influenced by events in Lesotho when the state of emergency was declared in 1970. It is a loose composite of real-life events that happened there during that period, and people who actually lived then. Many readers have commented that these events are very much similar to events that happened in a number of Latin American countries. Hence the play was translated into Catalan (for performance in the Barcelona region of Spain) and into Castilian. The hope was that the Castilian version would also be performed in Latin America.

The play was adapted for radio and was first broadcast by the British Broadcasting Corporation in 1992. The stage version was first performed in Johannesburg in 1995. It is a clear indication that the post-apartheid era has freed the imagination of the theatre practitioner. Now he is able to explore subjects and themes that are beyond the borders of South Africa, but that are still relevant to this new society here. This play has been variously described as a story of brutality in the name of democracy, and "a miraculous story — a story with its roots solid in the neo-classical revolution in Africa: Communism as against Western ideologies; the evil as against the good; the unstable existence of the church and the state ... as well as the first uncertain steps of 'democracy'" (de Villiers 1995).

Maishe Maponya is one of the pioneers of Theatre of Resistance, and **Umongikazi/The Nurse** belongs to that genre. It is agitprop theatre on the plight of nurses of South Africa and on poor health services for blacks. Its broad message is that the exploited black nurses should unite and form a trade union to fight for their rights. It is not divorced from the broader context of South African politics. It agitates for change. It does this in a highly original form, without using clichés or crude slogans as was common with a lot of Theatre of Resistance of the time.

A critic wrote: "**Umongikazi** was written in the wake of controversy about spending cutbacks and poor facilities at Baragwanath Hospital and portrays the world of the black nurse. It was scripted from 'talks and chatter' with people connected with hospital goings on, and was said to abound with 'wit, humour and horror', when it was first performed." (Leshoai 1984, 28)

Umongikazi/The Nurse is a play of the 1980's, when apartheid was at its most vicious. It would be interesting to compare the situation depicted in the play with our post-apartheid health delivery services today. Have things changed? And if so, to what extent?

Prof Z K G Mda
Westdene, Johannesburg
April 3, 1996

Ahmed, Junaid (1990) Culture in South Africa: the challenge of transformation **Spring is Rebellious** (eds. Ingrid de Kok and Karen Press) Cape Town: Buchu Books

Angove, Coleen (1992) Alternative theatre: reflecting a multiracial South African society? **Theater Research International** Vol 17 No 1

Brink, Andre (1991) **Towards a redefinition of aesthetics**, unpublished paper presented at the New Nation's Writer's Conference, December

de Villiers, Aart (1995) Baie bevredigende teater **Kalender**, Maart 30

Horn, Andrew (1986) South African Theatre: ideology and rebellion **Research in African Literatures** Vol 17 No 2

Kavanagh, Robert (1985) **Theatre and Cultural Struggle in South Africa** London: Zed Books

Langa, Mandla (1990) Interview: Albie Sachs **Rixaka** issue 1

Larlham, Peter (1985) **Black Theater, Dance and Ritual in South Africa** Ann Arbour: UMI Research Press

le Roux, Frans (1989) Theatre **Weekly Mail** January 13 to 19

Leshoai, Thabiso (1984) New Life breathes in 'Nurses' **Sowetan** October 25

Leshoai, Thabiso (1989) Theatre **City Press** April, 23

Manaka, Matsemela (1980) **Egoli: City of Gold** Johannesburg: Soyikwa/Ravan Press

Meintjies, Frank (1990) Albie Sachs and the art of protest **Spring is Rebellious** (eds. Ingrid de Kok and Karen Press) Cape Town: Buchu Books

Mhlophe, Gcina (1988) **Have you seen Zandile?** Braamfontein: Skotaville Publishers (also Portsmouth N.H.: Heineman/Methuen)

Minervini, Rina (1990) The heart is lost in the "Fever" **Sunday Star** April 1

Ndebele, Njabulo (1984) Turkish tales and some thoughts on South African fiction **Staffrider** Vol 6 No 1

New Nation (1992b) Playland **New Nation** July 19 to 30

New Nation (1992c) Forgiveness, reconciliation and JUSTICE **New Nation** August 7 to 13

Nyatsumba, Kaizer (1991) Theatre in a rut **Tribute** January

Pemba, Titus (1992) Good, evil, cliche characters **City Press** July 26

Potgieter, De Wet (1992) SADF hid suspects in Webster probe **Sunday Times** August 9

Ronge, Barry (1990) All trite on the night **Sunday Times** August 1

Ronge, Barry (1992) Fugard beacon for SA theatre's future **Sunday Times** July 19

Sachs, Albie (1990) Preparing ourselves for freedom **Spring is Rebellious** (eds Ingrid de Kok and Karen Press) Cape Town: Buchu Books

Thamm, Marianne (1989) 16 years on, a new look at freedom **Weekly Mail** May 12 to 18

Tonight! (1992) 'Playland' has its US premier **The Star** August 27

Watson, Ines (1994) play comes to life with music **Daily Dispatch** August 12

Wren, Celia (1990) Theatre of liberation or protest? It's still a winner **Weekly Mail** January 26 to February 1

SO WHAT'S NEW

a play by

Fatima Dike

SO, WHAT'S NEW was first performed at the Market Theatre in Johannesburg in September 1991, with the following cast of characters:

Doris Sehula
Pat Mabuya
Motshabi Tyelele
Nomsa Nene
Directed by Barney Simon

SO WHAT'S NEW

ACT 1 SCENE 1

The lounge/kitchen of Big Dee's house. The lounge is decorated in bold, nouveau riche style, a large couch with a matching two seater and armchair. A coffee table, a long counter which separates the kitchen area. Beyond the kitchen, through a beaded curtain, the storage area for Big Dee's shebeen is visible. The shebeen is beyond that, outside. Another doorway also curtained by beads leads to the rest of the house — the bedrooms, the bathroom. Downstage centre is the focal point of the room, a large T.V. set.

   Blackout. The signature tune of "The Bold and the Beautiful" comes up. Lights up. Big Dee rushes in, grabs a plate of raisins and settles in her favourite seat on the big couch. Voices of soap opera characters. Big Dee settles ecstatically, immediately absorbed. After a few beats Pat enters, carrying a battered brief case.

PAT: Hey, hello Dee I am fine thanks. What about you? (*Dee ignores her*) Hello Dee, I'm fine thanks, what about you?
Pat goes straight to the fridge to get a beer.
PAT: Tyhini ntombi ndiyakubulisa.
DEE: I'm fine Pat. (*Pat takes a big gulp of beer.*) Uyabona ke sisi, now you owe me R178,00.
PAT: Awu, Dee, khawuyeke, man! You are the richest she-been queen in Soweto and I'm starving. Yazi selling houses in Soweto can be hell. Hayi, I must find myself another job.
Dee laughs, still absorbed in the soap opera.
DEE: I told you to go back to showbiz.
PAT: And starve!
DEE: But you say you are starving anyway.
PAT (*Settling into an armchair*): Hey what's this? Is it Capitol or...?
DEE: No it's the Bold and the Beautiful.

PAT: Have I missed much?

DEE: You've missed everything.

PAT: Khawuyeke tu Dee! Indlel'endibaleke ngayo and the damn taxi got caught in the rush hour traffic.

DEE: Sshh!

PAT: I felt like killing the driver.

DEE: Sshh! Hayi if Caroline falls for Ridge's lies again, I'll puke, true's god ndiza kumnyanya.

PAT: Yo! When Caroline was raped, whose testimony saved her? It was Ridges! She owes him my dear.

DEE: Yabona wena, this is why I don't like you here. You always spoil The Bold and the Beautiful. You always mix me up. Caroline is smart, she knows that if she goes back to Ridge, he'll break her heart.

PAT: Ag, Ridge has learnt his lesson.

DEE: Khawuthule man.

PAT (*Teasing*): Sshh!

DEE: Thyini kutheni ngathi uza kunoliphata nge T.V. yam. For a moment there I thought she was going to give in to Ridge.

PAT: And she will.

DEE: Aga maan, Caroline is cool. Ridge won't get away with his bullshit. We women suffer but we learn.

PAT: Khautsho Dee, why is Caroline's father so anxious for her to marry Thorn.

DEE: I'd go for Thorn too, if Caroline were my daughter.

PAT: Ag Thorn is soft. He is the type of guy who would let a woman walk all over him.

DEE: And Ridge is a slut. He sleeps with anything on two legs as long as it wears a skirt.

PAT (*Laughs*): That's my kind of man. I want a man to sweep me off my feet, and when I wake up in his bed the next day, then I say, "My God, what happened, where am I?" I don't want a guy who will say, "Asseblief tog Pattie!" That's Thorn.

DEE: Hey, you want a sex maniac?

PAT: Don't you?

DEE: Hey nkazana, we were talking about you not me.

PAT: Hey I told you what I want from a man. What do you like?

DEE: I like them to be sexy and passionate and gentle.

PAT: Then we agree Ridge is sexy.

DEE: He's not my type.

PAT: What's your type.

DEE: Just shut up and watch!

They watch the T.V. for a moment

PAT: Margo is another reason why Caroline's father hates Ridge.

DEE (*Irate*): Awu Pat, uva xa kusithiwani?

PAT: Everytime she kisses Caroline's father, you can see that her heart is not in it.

DEE (*Watching T.V.*): Sshh!

PAT: Ridge and Caroline are still in love. I am a woman I know.

DEE (*Despite herself*): If she is, she is hiding her feelings very well.

PAT: Take it from me she is.

DEE: After what he did to her, ne? I'd stick to Thorn. At least he is faithful!

PAT: But what she shares with Ridge is strong. It will always come between her and Thorn.

DEE: Oh please Pat, don't talk nonsense. It didn't stop Ridge from sleeping with another woman the night before he was to marry Caroline.

PAT: Dee, you know men, you know them.

DEE: I know them, but this one has met his match.

PAT: He deserves another chance.

DEE: To get her into his bed?

PAT: That's up to Caroline. Deep down Ridge loves her.

DEE: Hu, Ridge loves Ridge, ask me I know men like that!

Pat laughs

DEE: Hey wena Pat, if men could have babies would they

sleep around as much as they do? Hey?

PAT (*Laughing*): That's an interesting thought.

DEE: They are too scared watching their own wives giving birth. (*Laughs*) Can you imagine what would happen if they gave birth just once?

PAT: Yo, they would use contraceptives just like us!

DEE: Not when they are lazy to use condoms.

PAT: Not if they knew they were running the risk of falling pregnant.

DEE: Ai suka, maan.

A commercial interrupts the programme

PAT: Hey I love ads. They give me a chance to grab another beer.

Pat goes to the fridge to get another beer.

DEE: Sisi yi fridge yam leyo ayiyoyethu.

PAT: Ag, I know it's your fridge but my favourite beer is inside.

DEE: Now you owe me R180.00.

PAT: Uyingoqo. What is your money beside my friendship? Where's the baby?

DEE: Mercedes? She hasn't come back from school.

PAT: She is late today and I miss her so.

Dee stands up from the couch and goes to switch the television off.

DEE: Eyona nto ke, Pat, I want to go somewhere. Willy took my car. I don't know where he is. I am supposed to go to the supermarket, to the bottle store, to the butchery, and I am sitting here wasting my time.

PAT: Did he know you were going to need it?

DEE: Hey nkazana, we have a standing rule, if he takes the car he has to check with me. Uyandi caphukisa ubona nje when he acts so irresponsibly.

PAT: Ag Dee, it's the rush hour.

DEE: Hayi suka, he knows about the rush hour. He knows he should be here.

PAT: But the car could be giving him problems?

DEE: What problems Pat? Huh? That car gets serviced every

three months. I'm the woman who pays, I know. I wonder where Thandi is? I could borrow her car and go about my business.

PAT: Hey, did you say Thandi? Is Thandi back in town? Uyazi Dee, I could kill that little sister of mine. My mother is forever asking after her, "Where's Thandi, where's Thandi?" as if I don't exist.

DEE (*Laughs*): Are you blaming her?

PAT: Hayi suka, just grab a beer and sweeten your tongue, it's on me!

DEE: You know that I don't touch booze during the week, and besides if Willy came home and found me drinking, you know what would happen.

PAT (*Raising her bottle*): Since I don't have a Willy, here's to life!

DEE: Wena, I've got someone to keep me warm, what about you?

PAT: Up yours lovie!

Both laugh.

PAT: Yazi Dee, I must still go home and cook, or else my son will divorce me. Suku hleka.

DEE (*Laughs*): I don't worry about that, Willy and Mercedes take turns to cook for me.

PAT: Yoo, if my son had a woman who made him cook, I'd throw the bloody bitch out personally.

DEE: Hayi Pat man, wena you are just jealous. If your son really loved the woman, he'd pamper her.

PAT: Hayi Dee that's my child uyazi, my one and only son. I am going to choose his wife.

DEE (*Laughing*): Come on Pat maan, Sandile is only twelve!

PAT: Uhu I can wait, I'll choose.

DEE (*Laughs*):   I feel sorry for her, who ever she is, akalibonanga.

Both laugh.

DEE: Hey, it's seven o'clock. That child of mine angakhe alinge nje andenze izimanga ngoba ndakumbonisa impundu zenyoka.

PAT (*Laughs*):   Why do I get the feeling that you are going to cook your own supper tonight?

Mercedes, sixteen years old, dressed in a tracksuit, enters through the kitchen door. She throws her school bags down on the kitchen floor.

MERCEDES: Hello Ma. Hello Sis Pat!

PAT: Hello my baby, your mother and I were just talking about you. How's school?

MERCEDES: School is fine, Sis Pat.

PAT: Aha!

MERCEDES: Ma, what's cooking? I'm starving.

DEE: Mercedes, what time is it?

MERCEDES: Has your watch stopped, Ma?

DEE: I asked you a question. Lixesha lokungena endlini?

MERCEDES: Cha.

DEE: Uyabonake ntwanam, in this house we have rules. If you feel you can't obey them, move out.

MERCEDES: Modimo, but Ma today is Wednesday. We have netball practice.

DEE: Netball practice my foot, Mercedes! If netball is going to keep you out this late, you'll have to give it up!

MERCEDES: Give it up?

DEE: Yes.

MERCEDES: But Ma, I've been picked to play in the first team.

DEE: Today your excuse is netball practice, tomorrow it will still be netball practice. You are still a baby. I don't want you dropping another baby on my lap. Your father died mtwanami without leaving us a cent. I want you to learn and make your own future. I want you to bring me a degree not a birth certificate, siyavana!

Pause. Mercedes gets her bags off the kitchen floor and exits to the bedroom.

PAT: Mmm, mmm, chom'am, kodwa, I think you are a bit hard on her.

DEE: Pat, what do you expect me to do? Hey? Ubona nje amaxesha ajikile. If I don't tell her now what's right and what's wrong tomorrow will be too late.

PAT: Amaxesha a jikile.

DEE: And so what?

PAT: Ha, today children know a lot more at an early age. If you are that worried about Mercedes, why don't you just take her to the doctor. Heh. You know what I mean.

DEE: And give her the green light to sleep around.

PAT: It's going to happen sooner or later.

DEE: Pat, just leave me alone wena man.

PAT: Sorry for butting in. Thanks for the beer, I must go.

Pat stands and puts the two empty beer bottles in a cardboard tray next to the bin.

DEE: Don't thank me.

PAT: Ag, just call it good manners.

DEE: Pay me!

PAT: One of the good days when I'm gone my friend you'll think about me. Bye bye Mercedes.

MERCEDES (*From the bedroom*):   Bye bye, Sis Pat.

PAT (*To Dee*):   Bye bye.

Pat grabs her two bags and exits through the front door. Mercedes appears through the beaded curtain and stands leaning against the doorway. Dee clears the table and goes to sit back on the sofa.

MERCEDES: Ma, why are you so angry with me? I've done nothing wrong. It's the truth. I've worked so hard to get into the first team. Please don't stop me from playing.

DEE: Come my baby. Iza ku mama, come, come.

Mercedes goes to sit next to Dee on the sofa. She lies with her head in Dee's lap.

DEE: Mercedes, when your father died mtwanami, I was younger than you. You were a baby. Your gogo was too poor herself to help me. All I knew to do was to sing. One day there was a talent contest at Eyethu. I went there with my friends. You were on my lap. And my friends said to me, "Come on maan Big Dee, go up. You are better than those people!" I was shy, but I went up. I just closed my eyes and I sang. (*She sings a few bars of a popular song.*)

Mercedes giggles.

DEE: Oh Mercedes, and the people clapped. Even you, you remember? Benny Moilosie of the Music Makers was there. And he said, "Baby, you've got the job". Ntwanami, I was so happy I was a Music Maker. That's where I met Sis Pat and Sis Thandi.

MERCEDES: The Chattanooga Sisters?

DEE: Ja, The Chattanooga Sisters. What a job! For five years, sleeping in a car, sleeping on cement. Two months no pay. I didn't know anything else. And then I said, "No more!" I went to work in a factory so I could have you with me again. Ja, my baby, and the men; it wasn't hard to find a man. I'm a woman who needs a man. I was pretty as you are. It's nothing I'm proud of. Do you think I am happy to run a shebeen with drunks banging on the door? Huh? I want something very different for you. I want you to be strong, to be clever. I want you to go out into the world and say, "I want this, I want that, I am my own woman!" If I fight with you, it is because I love you. You are the only good thing that has happened in my life. You have given me something to live for, my child.

Thandi and Pat enter through the front door singing a phrase of a popular commercial song, "Tambayi". Dee and Mercedes get up from the sofa to watch them.

PAT, THANDI AND MERCEDES: The Chattoonga Sisters! (*They all laugh*)

DEE: Thandi, Thandi, where did you get that suit?

THANDI: You like it?

DEE: Yes.

Thandi sings "Tambayi" and dances in a circle.

THANDI: Aha! I got it from Derbers, back door, exclusive!

MERCEDES: Exclusive!

THANDI: I can get it for you too. Girls I'm sorry, big business calls.

Thandi and Pat exit singing "Tambayi" and exit through the front door. Dee runs after them shouting.

DEE: Thandi! Which way are you going? Thandi, which way

are you going? Thandi!

Lights go down on Dee and Mercedes in the lounge watching the two women leave.

ACT 1 SCENE 2

Lights up on Sis Dee sitting at the kitchen table reading the Sowetan newspaper

THANDI: Hello Big Dee! No T.V.?

DEE: I didn't want to watch anymore. Caroline, that woman, she's breaking my heart.

THANDI: Willie's not here?

DEE: Don't talk to me about him! I don't want to know about him! But if my car isn't back by tomorrow, I'm going to the police.

THANDI: Hau, You'll get all of us into trouble!

DEE: That's your problem, not mine! Tomorrow I'm throwing all of his clothes out into the street, whoever wants them, can have them, they can have a jumble sale.

THANDI (*Laughing*):   Pierre Cardin. Yo Big Dee! I can see him running around in his underpants.

DEE: No, come and collect them! You'll make a fortune! I know what they're worth, I paid for them!

THANDI: I'm just from Armstrong. He isn't there.

DEE: Don't tell me, I went there this afternoon. Armstrong sat there like a Baby Huey smiling as if he was born yesterday… "I haven't seen him Sis Dee. I thought he was with you! I was just going to 'phone you!" Hey, I nearly klapped him! The way they were all looking at me I knew there was shit. If it's that bloody Thoko again — that bloody Miss Ellerines. I'll kill them both.

THANDI: I've been looking for him too. They said he was in Nelspruit.

DEE: Nelspruit! Kak! Because they told me he was in Germiston.

THANDI: What do you think I'm here for? I need him badly

too! There's a big delivery coming in from Botswana and we have to get it organized. There's more coming from Durban — I've got to clear what we've got.

DEE: Hey! I told you! I don't want to know anything about your business. I don't want to know about anything — have you looked at the newspaper today? Killing, fighting. Everybody blaming everybody else. I don't care whose fault it is, I just want it to stop! I want the whole world to stop!

THANDI: Twenty-four hours sleep could do us all some good!

DEE: It's not a joke!

Mercedes enters

MERCEDES: Hello Ma, hello Sis Thandi.

THANDI: Hello Baby.

MERCEDES: I saw your car parked outside.

DEE: It's half past six! What was it today? Netball? Where's your tracksuit?

MERCEDES: I told you Ma, the youth club meeting.

DEE: And your skirt?

MERCEDES: What do you mean?

DEE: Tomorrow you'll tell me that the school uniform is hot-pants!

MERCEDES: Ma, you said I could wear it like this.

DEE: Two feet above the knees? (*Thandi and Mercedes laugh*)

MERCEDES: Hai Ma, you want me to walk around like a holy sister?

DEE: I want your skirt to touch your knees!

MERCEDES: They'll laugh at me at school.

DEE: I pay, so you'll do what I say. Yesterday she brought me the list for her summer uniform — R400.00! You can thank God your mother isn't a poor domestic servant!

THANDI: In our day we didn't have a summer uniform, we wore one uniform right through the year; black gym, white shirt!

MERCEDES: Even in summer Sis Thandi?

THANDI: The same, black gym, white shirt!

MERCEDES: It must have been hell for you guys!

THANDI: It must have been, but we never thought about it. You know what, I used to sleep on mine.

MERCEDES: Sleep on it?

THANDI (*Demonstrates*): I used to put newspapers inside it and spread it out on my mattress and then another newspaper on top of that and then an old blanket and then my sheet. I used to iron in my sleep.

DEE: Ag, we all did that!

THANDI: Hey Baby, look in the boot of my car, there's something grand in there for you. (*Thandi hands Mercedes the car keys*)

DEE: I don't want her looking in your boot!

THANDI: No, its fine. It's in a white plastic packet.

MERCEDES: Okay Sis Thandi! (*Mercedes exits through the front door*)

DEE: You spoil her.

THANDI: I love her. She's growing up.

DEE: Don't tell me!

THANDI: I wonder what her father would say if he were alive?

DEE: He would be worried like me!

THANDI: I remember when she was born he said, "Thandi, this is my Mercedes Benz. The man who marries her will have to pay me enough lobola to buy a car like that."

DEE: Is he doing business in my car?

THANDI: Who?

DEE: Ooh, Willy!

THANDI: I told you, I don't know what Willy is doing, I'm looking for him myself.

DEE: And I'm telling you that, if he's using my car for your dagga, I'm going to the police station.

Mercedes enters singing and holding a red dress.

MERCEDES: Sis Thandi, hey Sis Thandi — it is beautiful.

She embraces Thandi

THANDI: Go try it on. Let me see you in it!

Mercedes exits singing into the bedroom and changes into her new outfit.

THANDI: Ag come on Big Dee, try a little smile. I've got troubles too.

DEE: What troubles?

THANDI: Hey Dee, on top of everything, my big bloody brother's moved back into the house and it's full of his friends.

DEE: Did his girlfriend kick him out?

THANDI: Yes!

DEE: So do the same. Good riddance to bad rubbish.

THANDI: Ag, stop it man. You know the house is in his name.

DEE: You pay the rent!

THANDI: The City Council doesn't care.

DEE: Move out, then he'll understand.

THANDI: Do you know how much I've spent renovating that house! A Jet Fire place, sliding doors, Italian tiles, burglar bars ...

DEE: Kick him out! Get some of your own boys together!

THANDI: I told you, it's in his name. We've just had a big fight! I told him — that food you're eating, that bed you sleep in, the blankets you sleep under, and that Russells sofa your friends spill their bloody booze on — I paid for them!

DEE: And what did he say?

THANDI: Fuck-off!

Mercedes enters wearing the red dress, her hair done punk style, singing.

MERCEDES: Sis Dee, How do I look?

DEE: Like you've seen a spook! It's too old fashioned.

THANDI (*Laughing*): Ag man Dee! Baby, you look sensational! I knew it was right. 'Phone Victor to come and see you quick!

DEE (*To Thandi*): Hey, hey, hey, mind your own business.

THANDI: What's wrong with Victor now?

MERCEDES: Ag Sis Thandi, leave it alone. Ma do you want

me to cook supper for you tonight?

DEE: Do your homework first, I'm not hungry.

Mercedes winks at Thandi then exits to the bedroom.

THANDI: Maybe she's hungry?

DEE: It's my house, it's my food.

THANDI: Yo, I can see that this is the wrong time to ask for a favour.

DEE: It is!

THANDI: Can I try?

DEE: At your own risk.

THANDI: I've got stuff in my car.

DEE: I thought there was nothing in the boot.

THANDI: I don't keep it in the boot. It's Willy's. Can I leave it with you until he comes back?

DEE: No!

THANDI: But he has to come tonight.

DEE: No!

THANDI: Oh Big Dee, I told you, my house is full of idiots.

Pat enters through the front door, throws her bag on the couch and goes to the fridge for a beer.

PAT: Hey Dee, what a day!

DEE: Now you owe me two hundred rand. And I don't want any stories at the end of the month.

PAT: Okay Dee — R200.00. What happened to Caroline?

DEE: None of your business.

PAT: Uh huh, she gave in! Where's Willy?

DEE: Ag go home, wena! Where's Willy? Where's Willy? You are asking me?

PAT: Dee, but your car's parked outside in the front!

DEE: And him?

PAT: I thought he was with you.

DEE: The bloody bastard!

Dee exits through the front door talking angrily under her breath to check her car.

PAT: At least your car's still in one piece! (*To Thandi*) Tell me, where is he?

THANDI: With Thoko!

PAT: How do you know?

THANDI: Armstrong told me.

PAT: Does she know?

THANDI: Nobody told her, but she knows. Armstrong said he was bringing the car back. I thought that he would be here. Oh please God...

PAT: You are looking for him?

THANDI: I've got some stuff to unload. Can I leave it with you?

PAT: Hau Thandi, for how long?

THANDI: I don't know. It's Willie's.

PAT: The bloody bastard, he's always full of trouble. Dee's right! She should kick him out.

THANDI: Ja!

Dee enters wielding red bikini panties and is furious.

DEE: Look at this! Look at this! Do I wear bikini's. Have you ever seen me in a red bikini? Is this my size? I'm going to get the Jack-Rollers onto him! I'm going to get the whole bloody police force! The keys were just hanging there for anyone to take!

Pat and Thandi start laughing. Dee exits to bedroom area. Mercedes enters through bedroom.

MERCEDES: What's happening?

PAT: Hau! We're banishing all men under the age of sixty!

THANDI: Only the old and the rich may remain!

They begin to perform the song "Ushugu — Daddy". Dee enters with a pile of mens clothing which she dumps outside the kitchen door. She joins in the number. They all collapse laughing.

DEE: Mercedes, where did you learn that? From your netball practice? Hey?

Light fades to blackout.

ACT I SCENE 3

Lights come up with them sitting with drinks. Mercedes is doing her homework on the kitchen counter.

PAT: Come on Big Dee, tell me what happened to Caroline?

DEE: No, never!

PAT: I was right, Ridge had her.

DEE: None of your business.

THANDI: I don't know how you can worry about these Barbie dolls.

PAT: Hey girls, let's phone them in America and tell them to do a soap opera about us.

THANDI: We're not rich enough!

PAT: You're rich. Big Dee is rich!

THANDI: Not rich enough.

PAT: All right, then it can happen in the future, in the new South Africa, when we're all rich enough. I'll be Patricia Mahambabusa of the Mahambabusa Estate and I'll organize a big sale that will appear on the front page of the Sunday paper.

DEE: To whom?

PAT: To you Big Dee! You remember that rich Italian? I'll sell you his house with the big garden in Saxonwold. Everybody will want it, even the big Americans. Ridge can be the rich American. He'll offer me the world, but I'll keep that house for you Big Dee. He'll make love to me in Sun City and on the beach at the Wild Coast and just when he thinks he's got it, I'll get that house for you Big Dee. You know, our friendship is worth much more than anything he can offer. Mercedes will have her own Mercedes Benz and she can have her own apartment upstairs with a separate entrance. And when Ridge realizes that I don't want him anymore, he'll go after her...

DEE: None of that.

MERCEDES: Ma!

DEE: Do your homework.

THANDI: She won't want him because she's got Victor.

DEE: No Victor!

MERCEDES: She's talking about the future, Ma.

DEE: Not even then.

THANDI: Will you still have a Shebeen?

DEE: Yes, of course. In the garden. Twice the size of the A-Train. Different levels. Jacuzzis and saunas for babalas. Nobody can come in with takkies and jeans.

PAT: No bare foot!

THANDI: Only tuxedos and evening dress.

DEE: Ja!

THANDI: And no cars below BMW.

DEE: Ja, no Golfs, no Toyotas!

THANDI: No Mazda!

DEE: No Willies!

PAT: You can decide that.

DEE: Eddie Murphy. He'll come and tell jokes!

PAT: And when he hears you laugh, he'll fall in love. They say he goes for Big Mamas!

DEE: Does he?

Mercedes laughs

DEE: Who told you?

PAT: About what?

DEE: That he likes Big Mamas?

PAT: I've got connections, my darling!

DEE: Hey, I like that man. He makes me laugh. He's sexy too.

THANDI: Come on girls, no more toy boys, we said no man under sixty!

PAT (*Looking at her watch*): Hey, my poor child!

THANDI: Where is he?

PAT: No, it's all right, he's with Ma. I'll go after Dallas, Hey girls J.R.'s getting engaged. (*Thandi exits. Pat gets up from the sofa and switches the T.V. on. We hear the title track of Dallas playing.*)

DEE: Mercedes, are you watching Dallas or are you doing your homework? If you are watching Dallas, go straight to your bedroom!

3 Gunshots are heard. Mercedes screams. Lights blackout for Mercedes' Monologue. Pat and Dee exit.

MERCEDES: What a night! When the shooting started, I was supposed to be doing my homework, but we were all waiting for Dallas, and Sis Pat was saying that J.R. is really sexy. Ma said that she liked Bobby better. Nobody asked me for my opinion. Anyway, when the shooting got worse, Ma switched off the lights and said that I must sleep with her in case Sis Pat wanted to sleep over, but Sis Pat wouldn't let us switch the T.V. off, because J.R. was going to have this big party. When we got into bed the noise was terrible. People were fighting in the yard next door. I said, "Ma, let's get under the bed!" And she said, "No, if I'm going to die, I want to die in my bed and not under it! You can do what you like." So I stayed with her. I never slept. Who is fighting outside? We were all too scared to look. Who knows? Does God even know? Is it the youths fighting with the migrant workers? Is Victor there? Or is it other shebeen owners fighting each other? Is it the taxi drivers? Are there white men amongst them in balaklava's, making trouble. Was it my fault? Did I say something that brought them all here? Was it the fight I had with Twana when I said, "We need education now!" and everybody else called me a sell-out? How far did the fighting spread? Where was Sis Thandi in her car? What if the police found her drugs and backdoor goods? Even when it was quiet again, I couldn't sleep. I heard the roosters and the dogs. I saw light coming up through the curtains. Ma slept through everything, how she does it I don't know. Just once she frightened me even more than the shooting when she screamed, "Get out of my house! Phumani man...phumani man" I shook her to wake her up and she just stared at me and said, "What?" And fell asleep again. Hai, sometimes I feel like my mother's mother. She needs taking care of, true's God!

Lights down on Mercedes, she exits. Lights up on Pat as she enters through the front door into the lounge for monologue.

Mercedes exits. Pat enters.

PAT: Hey what a night! I slept over in Mercedes' bed because there was no way I could go home. I was lying in bed listening to the guns shooting and when the shooting was at its hottest, my bloody throat decided it wanted a drink of water. I said, "Voetsak, you stay thirsty!" I was afraid to go to the kitchen in case someone saw me and took a shot at me. But my throat nagged and nagged and nagged. Finally I couldn't stand it anymore. I crept to the door of the room, suddenly it was dead quiet, I reached for the door handle and pulled it down very, very gently. It Squeaked! My heart stopped. I listened for a while, then I pulled the door handle down very, very slowly. Whenever it creaked, I'd stop, wait, then I pulled the door handle a little further again. This went on until I got the door open wide enough for me to crawl out. I crept across the lounge. When I got to the kitchen, the shooting had stopped. Then I realized that if I opened the cupboard to look for a glass I would make a noise. Instead, I bent down, covered the tap with my mouth, and opened it very, very slowly. I was still drinking this beautiful cold water when the shooting started again. I just ducked down and crept right back into Mercedes' bed. When the shooting was over, I just lay there listening to the water running.

Dee enters and turns the running water off. Pat is lying on the couch stage right — sleeping. Pat exits through the front door as lights go down on her and lights come up on Dee at kitchen door. Thandi and Pat enter from 2 front entrances completely covered in grey blankets. They both crouch on the floor in front of them crying.

DEE: I turned the water off this morning. Hayi! What a night. My house was surrounded by men. Men with axes and knives and guns. Men singing and shouting. They were banging on the doors and burglar bars trying to get in. I ran around the house closing the windows, but the men outside were pulling them open. I hit their fingers with this bottle and pulled the windows closed. Suddenly I saw two women on the floor crying and praying. They were terrified like I was. They were asking for shelter, but what if the men outside wanted to kill them? What if they smashed through my burglar bars and my doors and they came in with their axes and guns? What would happen to my child? What would happen to me?

(*Dee suddenly chasing them out one by one*)

Mercedes came running out of her bedroom screaming. I went to see what had frightened her. There were other men and women hiding in my bed. We had nowhere to go. Suddenly it was quiet again. There was a knock on the window, a soft knock. It sounded like a friend.

Mercedes runs to Dee and grabs her around her waist from behind.

I went to look out. There was a man with wild hair. His eyes were red. He pointed a gun at my head and he said, "Wait, wait…we'll get you all!" (*Pause. Dee sighs*). It was all a dream. What kind of a world is this that makes dreams like this happen in a woman's heart.

INTERVAL

ACT 2 SCENE 1

It is late on Sunday morning. A figure is sleeping on the sofa, engulfed by a blanket. Dee enters from the bedroom area. She is groggy. The phone is ringing. Dee complains loudly and answers it.

DEE: Ja, Hey? Who…? (*She answers the phone*) Why are you 'phoning so early? You got the wrong number, and even if it were the right number, she's still not here! Bloody Victor!

Mercedes enters from the back door with a bucket and rags. She starts cleaning the basin, then she sweeps the carpet and dusts the T.V.

MERCEDES: Morning, Ma.

DEE: What's the time?

MERCEDES: Quarter to twelve.

DEE: Why didn't you wake me?

MERCEDES: Hayi, Ma, what would you have said if I did?

DEE: Don't be cheeky. Why aren't you at school?

MERCEDES: It's Sunday Ma. You said the same thing to me yesterday, don't you remember?

DEE: Careful, or I'll send you to that convent in Umtata.

MERCEDES: Ma, I'm cleaning up. Doesn't that make me good?

DEE: You're getting clever, my girl. Those German nuns will fix you.

MERCEDES: What's a German nun like, Ma?

DEE: Very big, Very tough! They've got fists like Terreblanche!

MERCEDES: Do you want some coffee, Ma?

DEE: No, I'm looking for the Panado! It's gone from the cupboard.

MERCEDES: It's there by the sink.

DEE: That bloody Dixon! I told him I'm not drinking, so he says let me mix you my famous Manhattan. I don't know what he put in it, but it sent me to Manhattan and back! (*She looks outside the kitchen door*) Hayi, this yard looks worse after a Saturday night than after last weeks shooting!

MERCEDES: Don't worry, I'll get there too.

There's a call from the front garden.

PAT: Good morning, Ladies, am I in time for the morning service? There might be some good looking choir boys!

DEE: I can't stand it!

Dee sits at the table and rests her head in her hands. Pat enters and sees the body on the sofa.

PAT: What's that? Who died?

DEE: Hey, I'm warning you, you have entered a mine-field!

Pat points at the body

PAT: Not you, that!

MERCEDES: Shush.

DEE (*Seeing the body for the first time*):   Nkosiyami! Don't touch! Fingerprints, Mercedes.

Mercedes pulls the blanket gently from the head. It is Thandi sleeping.

DEE: How did she get there?

MERCEDES: I put her there.

PAT: When?

THANDI (*Eyes closed*): Six o'clock this morning.

PAT: Put on the T.V.! Maybe they're playing the Hallelujah Chorus! You bitch, where have you been?

Pat beats Thandi with the grey blankets. Thandi gets up and runs from Pat.

THANDI: Don't ask me now. I haven't slept for two days.

PAT: That's the best time to ask you. You drive off, the shooting starts and you disappear for a week! Where have you been?

THANDI: I heard Big Dee say she's been to Manhattan and back. I've been to Beirut and back.

Pat chases Thandi around the lounge.

PAT: Why didn't you 'phone me? Why didn't you send a message?

THANDI: Hey Sisi, I didn't think you cared.

PAT: Not me! Your Ma. She went crazy and she nearly drove me crazy. I had to take her to every bladdy police station in the book.

THANDI: Hey, no Pat. This is the day of rest!

PAT: Ja! Just think about it! With her standing next to me, I had to report you and your car, when I know you, what's in your car, and where your bladdy car came from.

THANDI: Hayi, no man...

PAT: We went to all the hospitals, even to the bladdy mortuary! I'll teach you, Rambo!

THANDI: Okay, okay, call me Rambo.

PAT: Voetsak!

THANDI: Danger follows me wherever I go.

PAT (*Lunging*): I'll teach you Rambo!

THANDI (*Running for the door*): Hayi, Mercedes, let me get some fresh air!

PAT: And I know whose car that was!

THANDI: What car? I haven't got a car anymore, I lost it when the shooting started outside the hostel.

PAT (*Sitting on the armchair*): It wasn't your car in the first place!

THANDI: And if one of that mob wasn't a friend of mine, I wouldn't be here either for your mother.

MERCEDES: (*Laughing*): Sis Thandi, do you want some coffee?

THANDI: Please, baby, black and strong. (*She heads for the sofa laughing*) So I go to Alex for the Botswana delivery and we hear that the drug squad are moving in to hit us. So we head for Pietersburg to meet the furniture trucks and they tell us they've also heard about the drug squads and the trucks are now in Mamelodi. So we ride to Mamelodi and while we're unloading the mandrax in the dining room chairs, and the dagga in the Edblo's another riot begins. (*She bursts into laughter*) Do you want to hear the rest?

DEE: No!

PAT (*Leaps to her feet*):   Put your shoes on and come and tell it to your loving mother! She thinks I'm a gangster and she's a hairdresser and my tsotsi friends have kidnapped her! I tell you — Cain and Mable! Ja! (*She crosses her fingers*)

(*Blackout*)

ACT 2 SCENE 2

That evening. Mercedes is on the telephone, she has the ironing board out and is ironing a shirt. Thandi is sitting on the sofa reading a Tribute magazine.

MERCEDES: Hey, I never got a message. Did you leave one? With who?… No, it's too much now, we're going to have a big fight one day — soon, very soon. No, but she must give me a message. Ag, no man Victor, she mustn't … no ja… I understand but she must too… Why don't you come here? She's out, she drove Sis Pat to Vereeniging to get her mother from a church meeting. (*Sudden announcement*) Do you know who's here? Sis Thandi! Ja, she's fine, she just suddenly appeared. She's sitting reading. What? *Tribute*! And she's just blown me a kiss.

THANDI: It's for him!

MERCEDES: It's for you! (*Laughs*) No, lots of adventures, lots of adventures, which I can't talk about on the phone. How long will you be? No, then it's no good, they'll be back by then. I'll come to you, okay? Okay … sweet … ja … bye. (*She puts down the 'phone*) Sis Thandi, he says he loves you too, I'm getting jealous wena!

Mercedes goes back to her ironing.

THANDI: Don't worry, feelings are mutual, remember our oath? Men under sixty! But he's a nice boy, he reminds me of Bra Sipho, a toy boy in my distant past, also a bright little face and white, white Adidas! I like a boy with nice blue jeans and white Adidas!

MERCEDES (*Laughing*): Hey, Sis Thandi!

THANDI: Did he 'phone this morning?

MERCEDES: Ja, he said so.

THANDI: I heard your mother, (*Mimicking*) You've got the wrong number, and even if it was the right number she's still not here! Bloody Victor!

They both laugh

MERCEDES: Hey, no Sis Thandi, it's not fair. He's always telling me I must understand her better. And she…

THANDI: What's she got against him?

MERCEDES: It's not him, Sis Thandi, it's the times!

THANDI: The times?

MERCEDES: When you run the street committee, Sis Thandi, how nice you are depends on the times. Remember how she used to brag about him when he started the cultural centre? Ja, you also came to that poetry reading that time, you remember, when I read?

THANDI: What do you mean "I came"? I gave you a nice donation too.

MERCEDES: Oh ja…(*Laughing*) Sorry Sis Thandi, ja!

THANDI: A big one.

MERCEDES: Anyway, now with all the violence and the gangsters, Bra Victor and our comrades are at war.

THANDI: What do you mean, "our comrades"?

MERCEDES: It's me too, Sis Thandi. I know your business, and now you know mine.

THANDI: Hey, I don't like it, I don't want to hear it, I don't want you to get into trouble!

MERCEDES: Now you sound like Ma.

THANDI: She loves you.

MERCEDES: I know she loves me, but when is she going to understand me? When is she going to understand me like I understand her? D'you know how many times a night men propose to me in her shebeen? But she sits and worries about who walks me to school!

THANDI: Yo! Tell me about this war of yours.

MERCEDES: Ag, Sis Thandi, you know mos, and anyway, I'm not allowed to talk.

THANDI: Come here.

Mercedes joins her on the sofa.

THANDI: Ag, you're so nice to hold! You're still my baby!

MERCEDES: You see, you're just as bad as she is.

THANDI: I just don't want you to get hurt, that's all.

MERCEDES: It's all right, I don't fight, I work.

THANDI: What does work mean?

MERCEDES: I look. I listen. We have meetings. We teach each other. We discuss the world.

THANDI: Yo! When you understand it, let me know.

MERCEDES: Ja Sis Thandi, I worry about you too. I wish you were a hairdresser.

THANDI: Can you imagine? (*Laughs*)

MERCEDES (*Stands*): Ja, I can. What about the Chattanooga Sisters? You're both still wonderful.

THANDI: With Pat? May the good Lord protect me!

MERCEDES: I hope He does anyway.

THANDI: Maybe I should have gone to this prayer meeting.

MERCEDES: I mean it Sis Thandi. Do you think about the things you sell?

THANDI (*Ironically*): Hey, no sermons, I was only joking about the prayer meeting.

MERCEDES: Do you know that some people are handing out mandrax for free in the schools?

THANDI: Since when? (*She stands*)

MERCEDES: They want to get us hooked.

THANDI: Not me!

MERCEDES: But you supply them! That's why I worry about you, Sis Thandi, because I love you. Now our war is against the gangsters... next it could be you.

THANDI (*Stunned*): Ja, the world never stops turning.

MERCEDES: That's what Victor says, Sis Thandi, but he means something else.

THANDI: Come here. Come right here.

Thandi takes Mercedes face between her hands and kisses her forehead.

THANDI (*Softly*): Mercedes Benz.

ACT 2 SCENE 3

Some days later. Shebeen noises from outside. Pat, in dark glasses, is watching TV. Dee bustles in through the back door and straightens her hair in the mirror on the fridge.

DEE (*Calling*): Mercedes! (*She notices Pat*) Hey, when did you come in here?

PAT: Ten minutes ago. I walked right past you.

DEE: Where's Mercedes?

PAT: She left two minutes ago. She said it was an emergency meeting.

DEE: Hey, I'm going to take a court order against that Victor!

PAT: Come on, Dee!

DEE: Why aren't you out there? Have you joined the A.A. or are you adding to your bill from my fridge?

PAT: Peace, Big Dee. I'm drinking water today. Last night nearly killed me.

DEE: There was a good looking guy called Cokes out there asking after you.

PAT: Hey. He's most of what nearly killed me!

DEE: He was looking for you so I told him he'd find you at home.

PAT: Are you crazy, Big Dee? My mother can smell a married man from a mile away. I'll have to move in with you.

DEE: Over my dead body! So, he's married?

PAT: Why, you fancy him?

DEE: Who wouldn't?

PAT: Learn from Caroline, Big Dee, love on the rebound is bad.

DEE: Who said anything about love?

PAT: I know you!

DEE: Where did you meet him?

PAT: At the taxi rank.

DEE: Oh, a true romance of taxis.

PAT: Something like that.

DEE: What does he do?

PAT: He drinks like a fish and keeps going all night!

DEE: No, I can see that. What does he do by day?

PAT: He says he works in the stock exchange.

DEE: Not bad! At least he's not after your money.

PAT: What money? And he didn't say what he did on the stock exchange? Maybe he's a messenger.

DEE: Could be worse! You dirty slut, you lucky bitch!

PAT (*Mimicking Dee*):   Ja, I've got someone to keep me warm, what about you?

DEE: Up yours!

PAT (*Raising her glass*):   Cheers!

DEE: Anyway taxi romances are tickey-line!

PAT: So you met Willy in a shebeen, what's that?

DEE (*Coyly*):   Who's Willy?

PAT: And if you want to know, he's been asking after you.

DEE: I don't want to know.

PAT: I thought you might.

There is a loud noise from the shebeen outside. A fight. Dee goes to the door and yells at the customers to quieten down.

DEE: Hey, if you don't know how to behave, you know where to go. (*She turns to Pat*) What? Did Thoko kick him out?

PAT: Who?

DEE: Willy!

PAT (*Laughing*): Who's Willy?

DEE: No! Come on man, did she kick him out or did he kick her out?

PAT: He didn't say.

DEE: Didn't you ask? I thought you were my friend.

PAT: Hey! Two seconds ago it was "Who's Willy?"

DEE: No, come on man.

PAT: I'll tell you if you'll let me off my bill.

DEE: You are asking to die!

PAT: Okay, keep your money. I don't want to die. Not tonight. He says he's missing you.

DEE: How much?

PAT: Like hell.

DEE: Good!

PAT: I think you should see him.

DEE (*Coy again*): Why?

PAT: I think he's in trouble.

DEE: Good riddance!

PAT: Are you sure of that?

DEE (*Despite herself*): What kind of trouble?

PAT: He'll have to tell you himself.

DEE: Let him tell Miss Red Bikini!

PAT: Ag, come on Dee, you know what Thoko means to him — goodnight — goodbye!

DEE: He chose her bed, let him burn in it!

PAT: Come on Dee, where's your heart? Boys like Willy burn quick.

DEE (*Pretending reluctance*): All right, tell him to come and see me.

PAT: He already has.
DEE: What do you mean?
PAT: He's waiting outside in the white BMW.
DEE: You bitch why didn't you tell me in the first place?
She runs outside. Pat laughs, watching her go.

ACT 2 SCENE 4

*Early that morning. It is dark. Thandi and Pat are sleeping in the
lounge. During the course of this monologue Mercedes wonders
about the room, opens the fridge, pours herself some milk and eats a
lemon cream.*

MERCEDES (*Laughing*): Hey, I go out and leave one Chattanooga sister behind and I come back and find two. Look
at them. Look how they're asleep. And they call me
Baby. What happened to them tonight? Sometimes I just
sit and think about the world, especially since I met Victor.
I think about all the people that there are, how many
people are there in the world? Yo! And I think ja, something is happening to all of them every second that passes
on this earth. If they're sleeping that's something. If
they're dreaming, that's something more. Right now, how
many babies are getting born, and breathing for the first
time? And how many old people are dying? And young
people? Hey, I've been to the funerals of lots of friends.
Funerals always make me cry but those are the worst. You
stand with your friends and cry for your friends. I've
stood by the graves of kids killed by the police, ja, and by
our own people too, and I've thought, "Hey, will I ever
leave this place. Will I be next?" Sometimes I've just
wanted to lie down with them, because it seems impossible that I will sleep in my own bed that night and wake up
and go to school the next morning. But that happens and
other things happen too. No second is ever the same. Does

everybody think about these things? Do white children?
They don't know what we know? What do they know?
I'm not sure. Do I want to know? I'm not sure. Sometimes
I understand about the world, sometimes I can't think
beyond my nose. (*Laughs*) You see, this is how I am when
I've been with Victor. When I'm with him he talks and I
listen. And I come back feeling like this. When I got home
I decided to tell all these things to Ma, but when I peeped
into her room, there was somebody in bed with her. Two
people snoring. I hope it's a man. I hope he's nice. (*Laughs*)
Shame, she deserves it.

ACT 2 SCENE 5

*Lights up on Thandi and Pat sleeping on the sofa early that
morning. Dee radiant enters from the bedroom in her nighty.
She is singing. They both wake. Dee links her words with a song.*

DEE (*Song*): Good morning ladies! I thought I heard
Mercedes.

THANDI: She's gone to school.

DEE: And why are you still here and when did you come in!

PAT: I couldn't move!

THANDI: I have been waiting for Willy.

Dee goes to the fridge to fetch the large coke bottle.

DEE: Well from today, I'll have to start charging rent.
Especially for you Thandi, because he's not coming out of
the bedroom for a long time.

THANDI: Ag no, Big Dee, this is urgent!

DEE: Nothing is urgent in this world. Have a beer or two
on me. I'll see you five-thirty for The Bold and the
Beautiful. I've got someone to keep me warm. What about
you?

Exits into bedroom
Blackout

ACT 2 SCENE 6

Mercedes is sitting in the kitchen folding political leaflets. Pat enters through the front door laden with a bag of gifts.

PAT: Hello, my darling.

MERCEDES: Sis Pat, Where have you been?

PAT: A weekend in Durban my dear. The Maharani Hotel, all expenses paid.

MERCEDES (*Teasing*): Who paid?

PAT: My loving sister!

MERCEDES: And how did you get there?

PAT: In one of my loving sister's taxis.

MERCEDES: Aha! And what did you bring back?

Pat puts a two-litre coke bottle of sea water into the fridge and gives Mercedes a necklace.

MERCEDES: Hey, thank you, Sis Pat! I'll wear it at the conference next week.

PAT: And watch your friends turn green.

MERCEDES: And what did you bring back for Sis Thandi? Something else that's green?

PAT: None of your business. Your feet are getting too big for your shoes, my girl.

MERCEDES: Sorry Sis Pat. It's not my feet that are the problem, it's my mouth. I don't know what to do with it.

PAT: Where's your Ma?

MERCEDES: Out shopping.

PAT: And how's the happy bride?

MERCEDES: Not so happy. Willy took the weekend off too. Don't tell her that I told you.

PAT: The bastard! He asked me to take the trip for Thandi so that he could stay with her.

MERCEDES: They were supposed to go to Sun City.

PAT: I know, I suggested it.

MERCEDES: She waited for him all of Friday night watching the pattern on the T.V. screen.

PAT: The bastard!

MERCEDES: I tried three times to get her to bed. We ended up having a terrible fight.

PAT: What's this? "Die eerste kaffer in my skool skiet ek vrek! Hou ons skole blank!" Who wrote this?

MERCEDES: Who do you think?

PAT: Look at the handwriting.

MERCEDES: We're organising big sit-ins all over the city, in every empty white school.

PAT: And the spelling? I'd think about it very carefully if I were you. I wouldn't let Sandile go to a school like this.

MERCEDES: It's not funny Sis Pat!

PAT: Have you applied for permission?

MERCEDES: It's still under discussion.

PAT: Yo! You kids have done your share, now it's about time you let your leaders do the fighting.

MERCEDES: The fighting?

DEE (*Off stage*):   Mercedes!

MERCEDES (*Grabbing the leaflets*):   Ag, Sis Pat tell her I'm sleeping, tell her I've got a headache.

PAT: A headache?

MERCEDES: She'll believe you. I had one yesterday after the fight.

Mercedes exits

DEE (*Off stage*):   Mercedes! (*Dee enters through the kitchen door.*) Ag no man, where's Mercedes?

PAT: She's sleeping. She's got a headache.

DEE: A headache? Still from yesterday?

PAT: I don't know from when. I found her on her bed.

DEE: Ag come and help me unload some booze for the back.

PAT: Where is it?

DEE: In the boot.

PAT: I'll help you just now. You look like I feel.

DEE: Hey, you know Sun city, it never sleeps! How was your weekend?

PAT: In Durban?

DEE: No, don't tell me. I don't want to know your dirty business.

PAT: Why not? Mission accomplished! There's a bottle of sea water in your fridge, compliments of the Indian Ocean and me!

DEE: Okay, have a beer, compliments of me!

PAT: So how are you otherwise, apart from no sleep?

DEE: Ag, if you've been to Sun City once, you've been there ten times. I told Willy next time I want to go to that place by the Vaal. How's Thandi?

PAT: Troubles with her brother! I showed her a house this morning.

DEE: And your Ma?

PAT: Fighting fit.

Mercedes enters from the bedroom and stands at the entrance.

MERCEDES: Ma? When did you come in?

DEE: How's your head?

MERCEDES: It's better Ma. I had a good sleep.

DEE: Come inside. I've got something to say to you.

MERCEDES: Ma?

DEE: I don't want you to see Victor anymore.

MERCEDES: Ma!

DEE: I know all about you and your plans.

MERCEDES: What plans Ma?

DEE: What plans Ma? This time I'm not joking about the convent in Umtata!

MERCEDES: I don't know what you're talking about, Ma.

DEE: I'm talking about your sit-ins! I'm talking about more troubles! I'm talking about you and the AWB! I'm talking about your bloody Victor!

MERCEDES: Sis Pat?

PAT: Mercedes, I never…

DEE: You stay out of this. I'm talking to her. You know who I met in the bottle store? Mr Sithole. He spoke to me about your plans as if I knew too. I was ashamed!

MERCEDES: Ma, do you let me tell you?

DEE: If you want to march, march out of this house and don't come back again! Come back when you've had your sit-ins and you're out of hospital. What's next? Where are you going to sit-in next? The men's hostel? Is your Victor going to protect you? Ha! Do you think I don't know about his plans? The whole of Soweto's laughing at him, he's going to fight the Jack-Rollers!

MERCEDES: Ma, let me speak!

DEE: You know who told me about that? Willy! He was laughing!

MERCEDES: Ma, he's one of them. Don't you understand?

DEE: Don't tell me about Willy.

MERCEDES: Ma, I don't care what you think you know, you don't know how to listen, so how can you understand? I am not going to change my life!

DEE: Okay, carry on, but I swear nobody will come into this house to tell me you are dead. Nobody will bring your dead body to this house. No prayers will be said for your departed soul in this house, finished! If you want something to do, take a broom and sweep the back yard, it needs it.

Mercedes sobbing exits through the kitchen door. Pat runs to the door. Dee sits facing the T.V.

PAT: Mercedes! Mercedes! (*She returns to Dee*) If you want to kill Willy, why kill her?

DEE: She wants to end up sitting here like me, waiting for 'Good Morning South Africa'?

Thandi enters through the front door

THANDI: Good morning? I thought it was good afternoon. And how was Sun City?

PAT: Nkosi yam!

ACT 2 SCENE 7

The three ladies are sitting in the lounge. They are singing and drunk.

THANDI: I'm telling you, that child is wise.

DEE: I told you, I don't want to hear about her.

THANDI: You know what our problem is? We don't think.

PAT: You're right. I was thinking about it the other day. I'm going to spend ten minutes every day just sitting and thinking. But everyday I forget!

THANDI: No, I'm serious, what I do is dirty, what you do is dirty!

DEE: And buys us bread.

PAT: And what I do is mad!

Thandi laughs

PAT (*Laughing too*): This morning after I left you I took a customer to see a house in Emdeni and the tenants chased us away with stones.

THANDI: Maybe we should all have our heads examined.

DEE: Speak for yourself.

PAT: Caroline went to a psychiatrist over Ridge.

DEE: And what good did it do her?

PAT: It's true! Who's going to cure you of Willy?

DEE: Shut up, wena!

THANDI: We're too old to start again. We're just going to live our lives out like this. I hope there'll be a nice old age home in the new South Africa.

DEE: Yo! I'm not ending up with you two.

PAT: What choice have you got? You just chased your child into the streets.

THANDI: Shut up! She's with her Gogo and she's fine.

DEE: What did she say?

PAT: That she doesn't want to speak to you.

THANDI: Yet!

PAT: I wish I had a child like her.

DEE: You've got one, and when he sees you?

PAT: Let's swop.

DEE: Doesn't she want her clothes?

THANDI: She'll wear her Gogo's clothes.

DEE: Mercedes?

*They all laugh. Thandi starts to sing. They all join in and end the
song laughing.*

THANDI: You know what she said to me? "Sis Thandi, why
don't you start Chattanooga Sisters again?" How about a
trio, Big Dee?

DEE: Hey wena, you two do what you like, I never called my
place dirty.

PAT: And who's asking me?

DEE: Ag, talk's cheap, money buys the whiskey. Phone Cokes
again.

THANDI: Who's Cokes?

DEE: Pat's boyfriend!

THANDI: Pat's got a boyfriend? Congratulations!

PAT: Congratulations, kak! He's got a nursing sister wife!

THANDI: And he's got you? Lucky man!

DEE: Come on, phone him. Maybe he's got some nice friends.

PAT: You phone him and talk to the nursing sister!

THANDI: Hey girls, here we are, black, single and successful.

PAT: Successful? Do you want to see where a stone hit me
this morning?

THANDI: Tula, big sister, I'm trying to propose a toast! Here
we are, black, single and successful and our love lives
are hell! Men pass through our fingers like water, and
those that don't are married, hangers on or just pure
scum!

PAT: Ja, men don't like women who own houses, drive cars,
have cheque books, pay the rent and open doors for themselves. We scare the shit into their pants.

DEE: I'll drink to that.

PAT: Just think! A week ago you wouldn't drink in case Willy
came home and smelt your breath. Let's drink to the liberation of Big Dee!

THANDI: I'll drink to that!

PAT: Hey, I must get home! Sandile will have to do with
Kentucky Fried Chicken for supper tonight.

THANDI: Tonight? He must be fast asleep.

PAT: Then I'll wake him! He loves it. Come on Thandi, drive me to the shops.

THANDI: I'm a danger to the roads and to myself. Try next door.

PAT (*To Dee*): Knock, knock, next door, will you please drive me to Kentucky Fried Chicken. I want to win back the love of my son.

DEE: Let me see. (*She gets up unsteadily*) I can stand, (*She walks around the table*) I can walk…

THANDI: Can you drive?

DEE: Am I walking straight?

THANDI: I thought you were driving.

DEE: I am. But I have to walk straight if I'm going to drive straight. (*She bends over Thandi*) How are my eyes? (*She puts on dark glasses*)

THANDI: Mmn, that's better.

DEE: Okay, now where are my car keys?

PAT: How should I know? I walked here.

DEE: If you don't know, just say you don't know.

PAT: I don't know.

DEE: Thandi, have you seen my keys?

Mercedes appears at the kitchen door

THANDI: I don't see your keys, but I see your daughter.

The other two turn to Mercedes. Dee takes off her dark glasses.

DEE: Nkosi yam!

MERCEDES: Ma, I don't know how my life began, and I don't know how it's going to end. I just know it is. I know I'm strong here, (*She touches her heart*) and I know it's because of you. I'm going to live with you and I'm going to keep on trying, until I wear you down.

DEE: Come here, mtanami.

MERCEDES: No, I've got to finish my homework.

Mercedes exits to her bedroom. Thandi and Pat clap.

Blackout

ACT 2 SCENE 8

The following afternoon. The T.V. is on. Mercedes and Thandi are sitting on the sofa. Dee is in the kitchen.

MERCEDES: So Ma, what's your conclusion? Will Brooke deliver Ridge's letter to Caroline?

DEE: Would you?

THANDI: Who's Ridge? Who's Brooke? Who's Caroline? To me all these white barbie dolls look the same.

MERCEDES: Brooke is Caroline's best friend and Ridge doesn't love her.

THANDI (*Confused*):   Who doesn't love who?

DEE: Ag, Ridge is just a dog on two legs, if he loses Caroline, which he will, he'll just turn around and console himself with Brooke. I know men like him.

MERCEDES: He's sexy, handsome and wealthy. I wouldn't mind him myself.

DEE: I wouldn't mind either, as long as he loves you only.

There is a knock at the front door.

DEE (*Shouts*):   Come in!

PAT (*Off stage*):   Hey Dee, why is the door locked?

DEE: These are dangerous times.

PAT: Come on, Dee.

DEE: And Wena you're the biggest danger.

MERCEDES: Ngu Sis Pat, Ma.

DEE: Nx, ag maan uyaphi, she's coming to make noise. One minute. (*She continues to watch T.V. There is another knock at the door, this time it's louder. Dee goes to open the door.*) Hey, voetsak man, this is not your house.

Pat enters. She goes and sits down on the sofa where Dee was sitting.

PAT: Why don't you kill yourself? I'm not going to stop coming here.

Pat sits on the sofa.

DEE: Hey, that's my place, sit on the armchair.

PAT: Hey, this is a bladdy shebeen I sit where I want to. (*To Mercedes*) Did I miss much?

A gunshot is heard in the distance.

DEE: Did you hear that?

THANDI: What?

DEE: It's a gunshot.

PAT: Gunshot? Now? It's too early.

THANDI: Ja, maybe it's a car back-firing.

PAT: By the way, what happened to Julie and Tyler? I missed Capitol.

DEE: I'm not talking till after Loving.

PAT: Okay, that's a promise! What did you think of yesterday's Loving? Poor Steve, he doesn't know his tail from his ass, Celia has him by the…

DEE: Poor Steve! He must make up his mind whether he loves Celia or Tricia.

PAT: Dee, you have a heart of stone!

DEE: Good, that's the way I like it.

THANDI: Hey man, let's watch.

PAT: Don't shout, I'm listening too.

More gunshots go off as if they are coming from a machine gun. Thandi gets up and closes the curtains.

THANDI (*Alarmed, to Mercedes*): Are the doors all locked?

MERCEDES: I'll check, Sis Thandi.

DEE (*Continues to Pat*): What would you do if you were in Tricia's shoes?

PAT: That's not the point. Tricia is not Steve's wife.

Another rapid round of gunshots go off. This time closer.

MERCEDES: What's going on?

THANDI: All clear, let's check the bedrooms.

DEE: Why must Steve stay in the relationship if he doesn't love Celia anymore?

PAT: Because he made a promise to love and cherish Celia till death. He made that promise in a church in front of a Minister before God.

DEE: I think that line is stupid. Nobody knows what's going to happen tomorrow.

Pat joins Dee on the sofa

PAT: To make matters worse, Celia is pregnant.

DEE: That's life, Pat, and there's nothing we can do about that.

PAT: Amen. Dee you have a heart of stone.

There is a loud explosion, it could be a hand grenade. The T.V. goes off. They jump off their chairs and sit on the floor.

DEE: Not again!

PAT: Oh shit! It's gone off.

DEE: Uyabona ke Pat, don't come watch soaps here anymore, watch them at your own house.

PAT: Hayi uyandigezela.

DEE: I meant it.

PAT: It will come on again.

DEE: Starting tomorrow.

PAT: Sis Dee, I've told you, one day when I'm gone you'll be sorry. What happened to Julie and Tyler?

DEE: Oh, no please, Pat.

PAT: You promised to tell me after Loving. There's no Loving now.

DEE: My life doesn't revolve around soaps you know, I've got other things to do.

A long battle between the two warring factions ensues. The women lie on the floor and listen.

PAT: Hey, this is serious. If I'm going to die I want to die next to my son.

THANDI: You stay where you are, or you'll get to him in an ambulance.

Thandi crawls across the floor and peeps through the window. Dee joins her.

DEE: Can you see anything?

THANDI: Something's burning.

PAT: Where?

THANDI: There.

Thandi makes her way to the bathroom.

PAT: It's the hostel area.

THANDI: What could it be?

PAT: They could be burning the hostels.

THANDI: That smoke is white.

PAT: Tixo! Teargas!

MERCEDES: Haai man! Victor!

DEE: You stay where you are.

Thandi lets out a bloodcurdling scream and runs from the bathroom.

THANDI (*Laughing*): The bathroom was dark and I saw myself in the mirror.

Mercedes crawls to the kitchen. The shooting continues. The 'phone rings, Mercedes moves to get up, Dee holds her down. The 'phone continues to ring. Dee crawls slowly to it, lifts it off the cradle and whispers:

DEE: Hello?… Who? Sellinah? Ja Sellinah?… What?…

She replaces the receiver back carefully and crawls back to her place on the floor.

THANDI: Who was that?

DEE: Sellinah. There are men outside the house.

PAT: Call the police!

THANDI: Don't make me laugh.

Dee gets up and goes to the window.

THANDI: What the hell are you doing?

DEE: They're stealing our cars.

THANDI: My car!

PAT (*Laughing*): Her car!

THANDI: Voetsak man (*Goes to 'phone*) Hello Armstrong…

The gunshots continue. Thandi crawls to the window and peeps.

THANDI: They're gone.

DEE: Our cars?

THANDI: No the men.

DEE: I need a man in this house.

THANDI: You need a gun, it's more reliable.

Fade to blackout

ACT 2 SCENE 9

Morning. Pat and Thandi are sleeping on the sofas. The 'phone rings, the women stir.

PAT: Answer, man!

THANDI: You've got two legs too!

PAT: Yours are younger!

Dee enters muttering

DEE: Are you cripples?

PAT: I think so.

DEE (*Picks up the 'phone and listens, curses*):   We don't want AIDS in this house! (*She slams the phone*)

THANDI: Hey, Big Dee, I thought you were nice to Victor now?

DEE: It wasn't Victor.

THANDI: Who was it?

DEE: Willy!

She sits smugly beside the phone. It rings again.

PAT: Hey Big Dee, pick it up.

DEE: Let him suffer!

The phone goes on ringing. Mercedes enters. Everyone is sitting up, wide awake.

MERCEDES: Hey Ma, what's going on in here?

Thandi exits to the bathroom.

DEE: It's a private matter.

MERCEDES: Maybe it's Victor.

DEE: It's not Victor.

MERCEDES: Maybe something happened to him.

DEE: All right. (*She picks up the 'phone*) Ja … didn't you hear me last time? … Okay! … One minute … (*She starts smiling*) Ja? … (*Her smile broadens*) Ja … (*Her smile broadens further*) Ja … I'll think about it!

She puts the phone down again, and smiles triumphantly. Thandi re-enters, drying herself with a towel. Pat goes out. She takes the towel from Thandi. Mercedes dials on the 'phone.

THANDI: What does he want?

DEE: None of your business.

THANDI: Come on Big Dee, your business is our concern!

DEE: After the way you run him down, why should I tell you? Stick to your own dirty business.

MERCEDES: Hello, Victor?

THANDI: You'll never let me forget that?

MERCEDES: Are you all right?

THANDI: What did he say?

DEE: I'll tell you in my own good time.

THANDI: That man is poison!

DEE: One girl's poison is another girl's plum!

MERCEDES (*On the phone*): Okay … ja … no, I was worried. Really … Yo! … no … Okay, I'll see you later. Come here … or I can come to you … okay …. sweet … bye.

She puts down the 'phone and smiles mysteriously.

DEE: What did he say?

MERCEDES: It was a private matter.

DEE: Hey wena. Umtata!

THANDI: More Zulus from Angola?

MERCEDES: More trouble at the hostel again. He's going to find out.

THANDI: So what was the "Yo!" really for?

MERCEDES: He was trying to get through but the phone was engaged.

Pat enters and goes to the phone and dials.

DEE: Okay! Now that you've suffered, I'll tell you …

PAT: Wait! Hello … Ma? … You okay? Yes, I'm at Big Dee's. Ja don't worry, she's here too, safe and sound. All in one piece, Ma. Me too, if you're interested. Is Sandile there? Did he have breakfast? Tell him to wait, I'm bringing him some nice Kentucky Fried Chicken. I'll see you. (*She puts the phone down. To Dee.*) Okay, shoot!

DEE: Would you like to now where Willy was last weekend?

ALL: No!

DEE: It just so happens that he was in Botswana and none of

the phones were working.

PAT: Yo!

DEE: He just got back this morning and he phoned right away.

THANDI: Phoned right away!

DEE: He heard about the shooting and wanted to know how we were.

PAT: And what was he doing in Botswana?

DEE: Attending a funeral.

THANDI: And what was in the coffin?

All but Dee laugh.

MERCEDES: He's not coming to live here Ma!

DEE: Hey wena, this is my house.

THANDI: Okay girls, I've got good news too! I've decided to buy a house! Let him keep the Italian tiles.

PAT: What house?

THANDI: The one you showed me.

PAT: Are you serious?

THANDI: Botswana's in! Durban's in! I can buy for cash! I know exactly how to fix it!

MERCEDES: Hau Sis Thandi, maybe there'll even be a hair-dressing shop at the back.

PAT: I don't believe it, commission at last.

THANDI: Who pays it?

PAT: Don't worry, it's the seller.

THANDI: Are you sure?

They begin to argue feverishly in vernacular about Pat's profession-alism and the intended improvements. This breaks into the Chattanooga song. At the end they collapse laughing on the chairs and sofas. Mercedes puts the kettle on.

THANDI: Hey, Baby, how about some morning coffee?

MERCEDES (*Pouring some milk*): The kettle is on already! (*She sits at the counter*)

PAT: Hey girls, I forgot to tell you about this idea I had. It's brand new.

DEE: About what?

PAT: You Sis Dee. It's called "The Rich and The Ruthless."
   Big Dee is this ruthless business woman, you know, something like Alexis, and she's after this toyboy ...

DEE: Ag, Dynasty is dead man!

PAT: Okay then say Thandi is like Margo, right, but a little
   older ...

THANDI: Older?

PAT: I said a little older ...

*They all begin arguing in vernacular with great intensity. Lights
begin to fade. The Bold and The Beautiful music begins to drown
their talk. Mercedes is laughing. There is a sound of gunfire over the
music, only Mercedes is visible. She is no longer laughing. More
gunfire. Music and lights fade on Mercedes' concerned young face.*

UMONGIKAZI / THE NURSE

An experimental play for two
male and two female performers

by

Maishe Maponya

UMONGIKAZI/THE NURSE

The play was first performed at the Donaldson Orlando Community Centre (DOCC) Soweto, in 1983. The performers were:

Gina Mhlophe
Fumane Kokome
Bennette Tlouana
Maishe Maponya

It later opened at the Market Theatre for three weeks and then performed to packed houses at Glynn Thomas (Baragwanath Hospital) with the same cast immediately thereafter. At the end of the third performance at Glynn Thomas, the writer was ordered to report at the Protea police Station for "a friendly chat", an interrogation by the Security Branch.

The play later toured Germany, Switzerland and UK orginally without the two leading performers, Gcina Mhlophe and Maishe Maponya who were being refused passports to travel "for security reasons". Sydwell Yola replaced Fumane Kokome.

Later performers in S. Africa included:

Thoko Ntshinga
Nomhle Tokwe
Oupa Mthinkhulu
Maishe Maponya

SETTING

Stage right takes only a third of the stage and serves as FEZILE's home. It is sometimes used as an exit area from stage left. Stage left takes two-thirds of the whole stage as the Hospital. When action moves from one to the other the Transition is indicated by a switch of lighting. Some scenes and episodes are flashbacks; these all take place in the Hospital.

PROPS AND COSTUMES

Two garden chairs and a small round table for stage right. A normal size table and a chair for stage left. A typical hospital screen, four chairs.

Nurses' white uniforms, matrons' uniform, theatre overalls and caps, khaki watchman's uniform and a knobkierrie, blue men's overall, hedge-cutter, shirt, white shoes, doctor's uniforms and overalls, stethoscope, surgical scissors, incubator, four pairs of spectacles (different kinds), two brown wigs, one Afro wig, newspapers (*Nursing News*), a big yo-yo, a brown file, small board with words 'CHEMIST' and two sticks at the edges to hold it, telephone, two white masks (different kinds), a hair brush, bucket containing water, soap, a washing rag, a walking stick, floral dress and a cap (for old woman), hospital pyjamas.

CAST OF CHARACTERS

The main characters in the play are

FEZILE: In his early thirties
NYAMEZO: A nurse. Twenty eight years old. **FEZILE's** wife.
MARIA: A nurse. In her mid-thirties
ACTOR FOUR, Portrays several characters indicated in the text.

OTHER CHARACTERS

MAHLALELA; DR LUMUMBA; BLACK DOCTOR; MALE NURSE, LOCAL SECURITY. They are all played by the actor who plays **FEZILE**.

PAEDIATRICIAN; PATIENTS (Sc 6); **1st NURSE** (Sc 6); **2nd NURSE** (Sc 6); **3rd NURSE** (Sc 5); **3rd NURSE** (Sc 6) They are all played by the actress who plays **NYAMEZO**.

OLD WOMAN; NURSE (Sc 1); **NURSE** (Sc 4); **MATRON; THEATRE MATRON; NURSE** (Sc 5); **MAGOGO, FLOOR NURSE** (Sc 7) They are played by the actress who plays **MARIA.**

WHITE DOCTOR; DR OWEN; PREGNANT WOMAN; QUEUE MARSHALL; PHARMACIST; 2nd MALE NURSE; POLICE OFFICIAL. These are portrayed by **ACTOR FOUR.**

SCENE ONE

BLACKOUT. Spotlight comes on an **OLD WOMAN** *singing an* **overture***; a background to the struggle. The song is entitled* 'Ntsikana *and is sung in Xhosa.*

Wayetshilo uNtsikana	Ntsikana has said
Wayetshilo umfo kaGhaba	The son of Gabha said
Ukuth'umzomnyama uyophalala	That the black home will be spilled
Ngenene wa phalala njengamanzi	And truly it was spilled like water
Wayetshilo wathi nothengisana	He had said that you will sell each other
Nithegisane nge qosh'eli-ngenamgxunya	Sell each other for the button without holes [money]
Amadoda ahlele ezinjwaleni	Men are now in the drinking places
Abafazi base marabini	The women are with the marabi
Kwenze njani na mzi kaphalo	What's wrong home of Phalo
Wovuswa ngubani xa ulelenje	Who'll wake you up as you sleep
Ahambile 'amaqhawe amahle	The beautiful heroes have gone
Ahambile ngenxa yo Mzomnyama	They have gone for the sake of the black home

Abanye bakufele wena Afrika	Others have died for you Africa
'Banye base mazweni bangamabanjwa'	Others are prisoners in foreign lands
Uyo vuka nini	When will you wake up
Uyo vuka nini we Afrika	When will you wake up Africa
Zayaphin'inkokheli zo mzomnyama	Where have the leadership of the black home gone
Ndi hlab'umkhosi	I am making a call
Ndi hlab'umkhosi ndithi vukani kusile	I make a call to say wake up it's dawn
Vukani kusile magwala ndini	Wake up it's dawn you cowards
Ndiyalila ndilel'umzomnyama	I mourn the black home
Ndithi ziphi inkokhelizawo	Where is its leadership
Holobanizikhali iyohlasela	Arm yourself and attack
Vukani kusile magwala ndini!	Wake up its dawn you cowards!

(END)

The lights come up slowly stage left on the **PATIENTS** *at the rear. The* **DOCTOR** *is visiting the patients in the ward. He goes from one bed to the other with sister* **NYAMEZO** *assisting in translations and other regular duties. Sister* **NYAMEZO** *is delayed at the back talking to one patient.*

DOCTOR (*calls*):   Sister Nyamezo, please come and help here.

NYAMEZO: I'm coming, Doctor.

DOCTOR (*goes to the next patient*) :   And who is this one?

NYAMEZO: Mandla, Doctor.

DOCTOR: I see… Breathe in, Mandla … Again … Okay. Open your mouth wider, … say ahhh! Ahhh! (*Examines him. Turns to* **NYAMEZO**) I think he's right.

They move away from the patients.

DOCTOR: Good Sister … I am satisfied with the progress of all the patients. As you heard, I may discharge about three of them tomorrow if their condition stays good. But, there is one patient I haven't seen in a long time … what on earth is happening to him?

NYAMEZO: Mahlalela, Doctor?

DOCTOR: That's right, sister.

NYAMEZO: He's always here at night. The sister I relieved this morning tells me he sleeps all night; but as soon as she knocks off and I take over he disappears. He was given his medication last night … here, look at his report.

DOCTOR: Remember sister, the patients are your sole responsibility. I want to see that patient tomorrow. Just imagine, I've had this ward for the past three weeks, yet I haven't seen all my patients. Make sure that I see Mahl-Mahl …

NYAMEZO: Mahlalela, Doctor …

DOCTOR: Never mind about the name sister … I want to see him! (*He rushes out*)

SCENE TWO

Early the following morning. **NYAMEZO** *bursts into the hospital ward only to bump against* **MAHLALELA** *who is already preparing to sneak out.* **MAHLALELA** *is dressed in hospital pyjamas, he has his personal clothes in his hands.*

NYAMEZO: Ja, and where are you off to?

MAHLALELA: To the toilet sister — out of my way I'm pressed, I'm in a hurry … Nurse kha undiyeke torho! [Nurse just leave me alone please] (*Tries to push past*)

Enter on-duty NURSE

NURSE: What on earth is happening here? What's wrong, sister? Why are you so early today?

NYAMEZO: I want to see a certain patient. I miss him every day because as soon as you knock off he disappears. The doctor wants to know what he is up to.

NURSE: Which patient is that?

NYAMEZO: Mahlalela.

NURSE: Mos nank'uMahlalela. [But here is Mahlalela.]

MAHLALELA: Leave me alone women, you are wasting your

time, I want to go.

NURSE: Where to?

MAHLALELA: Toilet! ... Since when do you stop patients from going to the toilet? Watch out ... I'll report you to the doctor!

NURSE: But the toilet is on the other end, Mahlalela!

MAHLALELA: I want to take some fresh air first before I go to the toilet.

NURSE: That's madness! What air? Go straight to the toilet or go back to sleep!

MAHLALELA: No one is going to tell me what to do. I do what I like here, I warn you women, get out of my way!

NYAMEZO: Remember you are a patient here and we are in charge of all patients. We tell the patients what to do.

MAHLALELA: Not me!

NURSE: You included!

MAHLALELA: If I lose my job because of late-coming you will lose yours the next day. Get out of my way; I'm late. (*Pushes them aside*) I am going to work ...

NYAMEZO: He is mad! We must report him to the Superintendent.

NURSE: Careful sister, you are risking your life.

NYAMEZO: Why?

NURSE (*narrating to audience*):   Mahlalela stayed on in hospital after he was discharged, that was three weeks ago. And every morning when he wakes up he goes straight to work.

CHORUS OF PATIENTS (*in the background*):   Fifteen thousand people have been on the waiting list fifteen years. No houses! Where do you expect him to live!

Exit all except NURSE

NURSE (*recalls as she laughs*):   And I know of a certain patient who apparently had an agreement with the doctor. This one was never discharged from the hospital because he had to clean the doctor's car every morning!

Exit NURSE *laughing*

SCENE THREE

FEZILE's home. Enter **NYAMEZO** *still dressed in her white hospital uniform — from work. On the small garden table are several copies of 'Nursing News'. Her attention is drawn to the very first paper with headlines which she reads out loudly to herself.*

NYAMEZO: 'Be positive, despite problems' (*throws it away and takes a look at another*) 'Call on S.A.N.A. members. Before you raise your voice to criticise the South African Nursing Association along with other uninformed people, make the effort to find out what the association does for its members; particularly in the area of salaries' (*disappointed at yet another*) 'A Christmas message from our President' very interesting (*stands up to read it carefully*) "As the year draws to a close, my thoughts go out to all the nurses of South Africa; who in this exceptional difficult year have served the nation with dignity, devotion and distinction. Have faith in your future — a better deal for nurses is just around the corner."

Enter **FEZILE** *in a happy mood.*

FEZILE (*with both hands clutched together, hiding something. He sings*):   I've got the world in my hands … I've got the world on my fingertips …

NYAMEZO (*getting more irritated*):   And what is that supposed to mean?

FEZILE: It's a song …

NYAMEZO: I know that, but what are you doing?

FEZILE: The conquest of nature by Fezile — a discovery. I am yo-yoing. First I yo; and then yo again … Thus producing a familiar repetitive motion known as yo-yoing … (*parting his hand to reveal long string with a yo-yo at the tip.*) … One of these days my name will go down in the history books of the world. How would you feel about it? Obviously great! And what is that supposed to mean? (*Gesturing at the papers with his head*)

NYAMEZO: What?

FEZILE: Papers on the floor!

NYAMEZO: Rubbish! Rubbish! I can't stand reading this paper these days. I often wonder why we have to pay subscription fees each year. It is as if the black nurse does not exist. Nothing is said about us and the progress we make.

FEZILE (*ignoring her*): Well I'm conquering gravity. Proving that what goes down must come up.

NYAMEZO: Will you stop that and start clearing this mess, if you don't want to listen — go and trim the hedge!

FEZILE (*continues with his yo-yo tricks*): I thought as much — look — look I told you. I'm conquering nature! (*sings*) I've got the world spinning and spinning at my command …

NYAMEZO: You are wasting time! Will you clear up this mess?

FEZILE: I'll clear it up after I've done this, my dear.

NYAMEZO: I know you won't.

FEZILE: I will. look at that skill! Makes me feel like a god. A movement of my hand and the world spins my way (*sings*) Give it a twist, just a flick of the wrist.

NYAMEZO (*peering at something she has missed as she went through the papers. Pulls the whole page out.*): Yes, this is where it all began, the whole story of the Nursing Council — all in one phrase …

FEZILE: Shoo! Ain't it funny? Keeps on going down and up again — I can't stop it …

NYAMEZO: I sometimes think you don't live in the same world as the rest of us. The only thing you are concerned about is that daft toy. Does nothing get through to you? Does your mind drift through your head like foggy smoke with no direction, no purpose?

FEZILE continues to yo-yo.

FEZILE: You should relax, my darling …

NYAMEZO (*irritated*): You don't understand, just put that thing away?

FEZILE: It is a cord. An umbilical cord between me and peace …

NYAMEZO: Some rubbish cord!

FEZILE: Well it keeps me alive … (*still yo-yoing*)

NYAMEZO moves out angrily. She comes back with a pair of hedge-cutters and in a split second cuts the string of the yo-yo leaving FEZILE with his mouth open in disbelief. Silence.

NYAMEZO: With that out of the way you will probably listen to me!

FEZILE: Damn it! I have no spare string.

NYAMEZO: Thank God for that.

FEZILE: I shall mend it. Though it will never be the same again because the knot will make it jerk.

NYAMEZO: At least you will now have to listen to me!

FEZILE (*getting a new idea*): Wait a minute. I am going to devise a new trick. This time I won't have to use a string. And you know what? Some mad-caps around the world will be identifying it as an unidentified flying object … I'm going to do it. I'm telling you … (*He wants to leave*)

NYAMEZO: All I'm telling you now is to go and trim the hedge! What kind of husband are you. It's toys, toys … an old man like you. You should be ashamed of yourself!

FEZILE picks up the cutters and reluctantly starts to trim the hedge. NYAMEZO picks up another 'Nursing News' and begins to read. FEZILE continues to trim the hedge.

NYAMEZO: Fezile! Fezi … ! Do you know that Dr Lumumba has resigned?

FEZILE: What?

NYAMEZO: Yes, he is leaving at the end of this month. Apparently he is leaving the country too.

FEZILE: Rubbish! I can't believe it.

NYAMEZO: "Rubbish! I can't believe it". It's here in this useless paper. I understand his reasons though … how can they expect him to drive all the way from Benoni to Atteridgeville in that old "Skodonk" every day, that's wrong! They should give him transport allowance. Not only that …

*FLASHBACK. Enter a **WHITE DOCTOR** giving information to trainees.*

WHITE DOCTOR: Look, working in this place you've got all the advantages on earth. A good salary — a really good salary, you attend to only a few patients like of course in the white hospitals. Granted there is congestion everywhere in the black hospitals, but you have all those sisters who have done primary health care to assist you. They are always around. You will get travelling allowance no matter where you come from. We don't expect you to come all the way from Cape Town for work. And another advantage is that you are a white-doctor-in-a-black hospital ... Ever thought of that! Yes, tolerance fee! I presume that we are serving a different community group ... that is our compensation ... Tolerance fee!

END OF FLASHBACK

NYAMEZO: Yes but these are precisely the reasons for his resignation. You see, apartheid is rooted in the hospitals too. Dr Lumumba was the first to realise this and he made us aware of it. Oh, how I'm going to miss those moments when Dr Lumumba would call us like a father to his children.

Exit **FEZILE.** **NYAMEZO** *moves to stage left. FLASHBACK. Enter* **FEZILE** *as Dr Lumumba.*

DR LUMUMBA (*calling out to* **NYAMEZO**):   Sister! Sister! Nyamezo!

NYAMEZO: Yes doctor.

DR LUMUMBA: Listen. Whether you accept it or not, the truth is right in front of you. Whilst we appreciate the progress you as nurses are making, we are not blind to the fact that this move is not only to alleviate the pressure in the clinics. No! It's also an economic strategy by the department of health. None of us is getting what the white doctors get and we examine the patients just as well as they do.

NYAMEZO: But Dr Lumumba, it's an opportunity we have to grab. At the end of it we'll know what every doctor knows ...

DR LUMUMBA (*raises his voice*):   That doesn't make you a doctor. Why train a lot of health workers instead of educating people. It's ridiculous — out of 23 million black people how many qualified black doctors have we got in the country — less than 4 000. And out of five million whites how many qualified white doctors are there? More than 12 000! The education system is rotten! And once you've come to this conclusion — you must start suspecting the teacher, suspect the book he reads from, suspect the school principal, the regional inspector and the whole bloody education system ... !

NYAMEZO (*shocked*):   Dr Lumumba! (*Exits to reappear stage right*)

DR LUMUMBA (*softer and slower*):   Yes, frustration of the black mother frustrates the black child and the result is a social breakdown of black life — that's why we have what they call in our schools "drop-outs"!

Exit DR LUMUMBA. END OF FLASHBACK

NYAMEZO: That was the man — Dr Lumumba. To think that he is no longer with us. He used to smart every nurse's ear with wisdom. He would say this in front of everyone. He would even say it to the officials ...

FEZILE (*still backstage*):   Hai! hai! hai! Would he have said it in the presence of whites?

NYAMEZO: What whites? Aren't whites officials? Oh, how we used to admire his convictions! And now to think that he's gone; what a loss!

FEZILE comes out with a bucket full of water, and soap all over head and face.

FEZILE: Now I see Dr Lumumba has chosen a wrong profession.

NYAMEZO: That is the man who has given me the right education ...

FEZILE: Wrong education. That man is not supposed to be a doctor.

NYAMEZO: His education was spiritually uplifting ...

FEZILE: Wrong education …
NYAMEZO: Right education!
FEZILE: I'm telling you that kind of education is wrong …
NYAMEZO: That's the right education!
*Enter **MARIA** as they continue to scream at each other*

SCENE FOUR

MARIA: Hi Nyamezo! Hi Fezile!
NYAMEZO & FEZILE (*surprised*): Hi Maria hi!
NYAMEZO: Long time no see Maria. Where have you been, what's up?
MARIA: Nyamezo, I am the most disillusioned nurse in the country. Things are bad for me, I'm out of work again.
NYAMEZO: Come now Maria, we are busy discussing something serious about Dr Lumumba and here you come with one of your silly jokes.
MARIA: Serious, I've lost my job.
FEZILE: Come on Maria, not so long ago you were telling us how nice it was to be working in the white hospitals … and so what's gone wrong?
MARIA: Yes, Fezi, but remember greener pastures are always full of snakes. Terrible snakes! The other nurses are still there but it's going to become very difficult for them there. Nowadays, the black nurses are put at the mercy of people we never thought mattered a lot in the hospitals.
NYAMEZO: Like?
MARIA: Like the white cook of course. (*NYAMEZO and FEZILE burst out laughing*). Just imagine a fat white woman who has no inkling of what it is like to be a nurse, exercising her unprofessional status on a black qualified nurse. "I will fire you! I will fire you, my girl! If you don't know how to behave in front of your seniors, this is not the place to learn that! I'm your senior and I will bloody fire you!"
NYAMEZO (*laughing*): Is that what happens?

MARIA: For God's sake! To think she's got an apron and I've got epaulettes and bars to show status, but to her status is this, (*indicating her cheeks*) and the thing that makes me mad is that we are barred from attending to some patients because there is a general complaint from the patients that they don't feel safe when they are attended to by black nurses.

FEZILE: Ja Maria, to expect to work harmoniously with the white nurses is impossible. It won't work. Just won't work! You see we come from different places, different homes and different cultures and apartheid has damaged the minds of the white people. The only thing that puts them together is the iron hand!

NYAMEZO: Exactly!

MARIA: To rub salt into the wound; black nurses at Wenela Hospital are now being instructed to leave their uniforms behind when they knock off.

NYAMEZO: Why, so they are not seen to be working there?

MARIA: Precisely. You know we are treated like assistant nurses in the white hospitals. When the white hospital nurses are scrubbing ...

FEZILE: Come on Maria, do you want to tell us white nurses scrub floors too? No we can't believe this one.

MARIA: No Fezi ... I don't mean that. What I mean is that when they are in the middle of an operation ...

FEZILE: Oh I see, that's hospital terminology ...

MARIA: Yes Fezi. This is not a layman's language. What I mean is that when they are in the middle of an operation, I, qualified as I am, have to wait on the sidelines and take instructions from them ... And the other thing that really made me mad was when I discovered their 'skinder-hoekie'! [gossip corner!]

NYAMEZO: A what?

MARIA: Yes, a 'skinder-hoekie.' You know, they keep a 'skinder-boek.' [gossip-log.]

FEZILE: Maria tell us why they call it a 'skinder-boek'. What a name!

MARIA: Because that's where they sharpen their scalpels!

FEZILE (*shocked*): Scalpels. Shoo! That's a dangerous weapon. Hai, white people in this country are a "disaster" to black people.

He exits with the bucket and comes back with a hair brush in his hand.

MARIA: Sister Nyamezo, I think I am going to rejoin the black hospitals. I will learn to tolerate the attitudes of other black nurses and black patients, after all they are my people and I understand them.

NYAMEZO: It's high time you did.

MARIA: I think I have to go now. Bye!

Exit MARIA. FEZILE *continues to brush his hair whilst looking himself up and down in the mirror.*

NYAMEZO: Poor Maria ... To think she was so excited when she was going to this white hospital of hers. And now she's back. Just imagine the white cook ...

FEZILE: All right, all right let's forget about Maria for the time being ...

NYAMEZO: Yes.

FEZILE: I've some business to talk to you about.

NYAMEZO: Some business? Aren't we getting serious these days ...

FEZILE: Yes we are getting serious.

NYAMEZO: Come, tell me what's the business about?

NYAMEZO (*quickly*): Remember the project I told you about?

NYAMEZO: A project? I can't remember talking to you about a project.

FEZILE: Damn it, can't you remember the other day when you asked me to trim the hedge?

NYAMEZO: Yes, I remember asking you to trim the hedge.

FEZILE: Ja, that very same day I told you about the project.

NYAMEZO: What kind of project is that? In fact I can't even imagine you involved in a project.

FEZILE: Well you had better start imagining it now. .

NYAMEZO: All right tell me, what kind of a project is it?

FEZILE (*getting irritated*): It's a project!

NYAMEZO: Ja, I know it's a project but what kind of project is it?

FEZILE: I need some cash.

NYAMEZO: What for?

FEZILE: For the project.

NYAMEZO: I know, but what is the project?

FEZILE: I need to buy some machinery. It's actually a fuel injection carburettor. Do you know what it is … ?

NYAMEZO: Fuel injection carburettor, what a beautiful name for a project.. But you still haven't told me what the project is. Isn't it boring for me to keep asking what is the project, what is the project, and still I can't get an answer.

FEZILE (*doubtful*):   Well … you know that I am inventing a new … Hmm … yo-yo.

NYAMEZO: What? A yo-yo. Do you seriously mean you expect me to give you money for a yo-yo! A toy! That'll be the day! Andi soze! [I won't] (*walks out of the house*)

FEZILE (*angrily*): Hei wena mfazi [Hey woman] give me some money! If you don't want to give me money bring back my whole pay-packet I gave you last Friday — I want my money!

He follows her.

SCENE FIVE

*In the casualty theatre for minor cases like circumcision, skin graft or tooth extraction. A **FLOOR NURSE** peeps through the screen.*

FLOOR NURSE: (*to the audience*) We were only left with five minutes to finish the case …

(**DR OWEN** *enters. The* **FLOOR NURSE** *comes out from behind the screen with some instruments. She bumps into* **DR OWEN**, *and the instruments fall to the floor. Dr Owen instructs her to pick them up.*)

DR OWEN (*puzzled*): And now, what's going on in my theatre?

FLOOR NURSE: We are busy on a case Doctor.

DR OWEN: I want an answer from the surgeon.

FLOOR NURSE: That won't help. All cases must be booked.

DR OWEN (*angry*): But I always get preference, you small banana.

FLOOR NURSE (*fuming*): Not this time, you big orange!

DR OWEN: You don't call me a big orange, you stupid!

NYAMEZO (*peeping from the screen and interrupting*): And I never realised there were oranges and bananas working here!

FLOOR NURSE: Neither did I, but I've been trying to tell Doctor Owen that we are busy on a case!

NYAMEZO: And how does he react to that?

FLOOR NURSE: You know this silly doctor has a bad tendency of bullying us around here in the theatre. He even goes to the extent of beating up the patients. He is really getting on my nerves.

DR OWEN (*pulls out a gun*): I'll shoot you!

NYAMEZO (*bravely*): That'll be the day …

DR OWEN: I'll shoot you too!

FLOOR NURSE: Do it now …

Exit **DR OWEN** *to call the* **MATRON.**

NYAMEZO (*agitated*): A whole doctor pointing a gun at us! I'm going to report this matter to the Nursing Council!

The NURSE rushes out. She returns as the **MATRON,** *closely followed by* **DR OWEN,** *to confront* **NYAMEZO.**

MATRON (*not even waiting for her side of the story*): Sister! It's indecent to talk so arrogantly to the doctor. Remember that he has sacrificed years of his life for this hospital.

NYAMEZO: If you talk to me in that attitude I will not waste my breath!

DR OWEN: Hear, I told you. This is the kind of people the hospitals employ these days, cheeky! I will report this matter to the chief matron! You are not solving my problem either!

He pulls the **MATRON** *by the hand.*

MATRON: Don't pull me so hard, doctor!

The **MATRON** *exits and returns as* **THEATRE MATRON**. *She has hardly opened her mouth to speak when* **DR OWEN** *starts.*

DR OWEN (*still angry*): These little bananas have a tendency of calling me names!

NYAMEZO: There he goes again calling us ...

DR OWEN: Shut up!

T. MATRON (*to* **NYAMEZO**) Sister, where were you in nineteen seventy six?

NYAMEZO: Don't crack your skull ... I had already begun working here!

T. MATRON: Well, here we don't behave like the nineteen seventy six children!

DR OWEN: Bloody terrorists!

T. MATRON: And remember sister ... I am going to write a report about your unprofessional behaviour ... I'm going to do it!

DR OWEN: I like your attitude Matron ... these nurses need discipline.

T. MATRON: Thank you, doctor ...

Exit **DR OWEN** *and* **THEATRE MATRON**.

SCENE SIX

FEZILE's home. Once more he is seen with a yo-yo in his hands. He seems quite happy with life while something is seriously bothering **NYAMEZO**.

FEZILE: Lovie wee!

NYAMEZO: Hee-

FEZILE: I have trimmed the hedge ...

NYAMEZO: Ja I saw that ...

FEZILE: And did you see where I planted the lilac flowers? It makes the view better, doesn't it? Lovie you know what?

NYAMEZO: Ja!

FEZILE: You don't look too good today ...

NYAMEZO: I know.

FEZILE: But you didn't tell me why?

NYAMEZO: How can I talk sense to you when that daft toy still occupies your mind.

FEZILE: Okay then, dear, I'm listening.

NYAMEZO: I think I'm going to quit!

FEZILE: Quit what now!

NYAMEZO: Just this morning I had a terrible experience at the hospital ...

Transition. A wordless song while the performers change costumes. A delivery room at the hospital; **NYAMEZO** *offstage as a WHITE SENIOR* **PAEDIATRICIAN;** *a WOMAN lying on the table is giving birth.*

NURSE (*to woman*):   C'ammon sisi, push — push — again — push! All right, all right hold it! (*taking scissors to cut umbilical cord*) Let's see how much it weighs? No! 850 grams but it has life — it will live. (*She puts the child in an incubator and goes out shouting*) Let me rush for the paediatrician. Doctor! Paediatrician! ...

PAEDIATRICIAN: Yes, what is it?

NURSE: We have a premature baby weighing only 850 grams ... but it's alive!

PAEDIATRICIAN (*peeps out the half open door*):   Ag! ... let it die man, it's got no chance anyway. Take that thing to the sluice room.

NURSE: But, doctor, can't we save it?

The paediatrician ignores her. A pause.

NURSE (*to audience*):   One hour later I went to clean the sluice room only to find it gasping for air. (*Speaks to herself*) It's alive! Let me rush for the paediatrician! (*runs*) paediatrician! paediatrician! You've got to resuscitate please!!

PAEDIATRICIAN (*reluctantly*):   ... Right! I am giving life to this thing and tomorrow it'll be the one that will snatch my bag!

(Voices of nurses can be heard singing in the background.)

'Senze ntoni na?'   [What have we done?]
Senze ntoni na?
Senze ntoni na?
Ho-ho-ho
Ho-ho-ho
Senze ntoni na?
Ho-ho-ho-ho-ho-ho
Transition — FEZILE's home.

FEZILE: … And what happened?

NYAMEZO: The child had already developed hypothermia and it died!

FEZILE (*shattered*):   Hayi man!

NYAMEZO: There were no questions. No investigations and nobody will be taken to task.

FEZILE: What do the nurses say about it?

NYAMEZO: The nurses fear victimisation, all they can do is lament. It is in fact, against the codes of conduct for me to give you this information.

FEZILE (*contemptuously*):   Rubbish. Codes of Conduct! The nurses must stand up! The nurses must be organised! All those racists must be pulled out of our hospitals. To hell with codes of racist conduct!

NYAMEZO: It's just such a pity …

FEZILE: What is a pity?

NYAMEZO: Dr Lumumba has left.

FEZILE: But you are there and every dedicated nurse is there! You should shout in one voice!

NYAMEZO: We cannot, because we do not have a union. The South African Nursing Association would be against it.

FEZILE: That very association consists of racist mentality — how can they take action against their own brothers? You should form your own union, go for it! Don't be afraid!

NYAMEZO: I won't be. I will go for it!

FEZILE: If you do that, I will be right next to you. And you know what my next step is going to be?

NYAMEZO: Yes, buy another yo-yo!

FEZILE: No-ways my dear ... I will give up my yo-yo adventures. (*NYAMENZO looks surprised*) Can't believe it? It's true. I will give up my yo-yo adventures! (*Grabbing the yo-yo to throw it away, while shouting with* **NYAMEZO** *close behind him.*)

FEZILE & NYAMEZO: Away with the yo-yo! Away with the yo-yo! Away! (*They continue to make noise back-stage.*)

SCENE SEVEN

The hospital. There is a long queue of patients.

QUEUE MARSHALL (*angry with patients*):   Msindo! (*looks down*) And now whose card is this! Kha u bheke! [Just look!] (*calls out the name out loud*) Jonas Magugane! Jonas Magugane c'ammon come for your card. Hurry up! Give him way, let him pass — take! Damn it! You are in the wrong queue. Don't argue with me ngi zaku phihliza jong! [I will clobber you!] (*Threatens to hit her*) And remember this is not an old age home. Hamba! [Go!]

Enter a nurse played by **NYAMEZO** *to confront a patient. The patient is imaginary.*

NURSE (*to patient*):   Yes? ... You come all the way from the gate to ask me questions? Who told you I'm the information officer? You must go back to the enquiries and there, you can ask them as many questions as you want. That's what they are there for. (*Turns and freezes with back towards audiences*)

Enter **MAGOGO,** *an old woman.*

MAGOGO: We phoyisa, [*policeman,*] do you mean I must stand in that long queue?

Q. MARSHALL: I can't help it salukazi, you must wake up. Do you think this is the pass office where there is a lot of bribery?

Phone rings. **NYAMEZO** *still plays nurse.*

SECOND NURSE (*rushing to answer*):   Hallo, hallo! Yes. Can I help you? (*Pause*) Hi Joey! (*Excitedly*) How are you, my lover-boy? Oh, I'm fine as usual. What? Pardon? I can't hear you. Just hold on a minute. (*Turns around to scream at a patient*) You are making a noise! I say you are making a noise! An old man like you crying from pain? Look at the blood! Are you trying to paint this place red? Rubbish! You must have been drunk when you had that accident! C'ammon move it! (*Back to phone*) I'm sorry Joey, you know these patients can really drive you up the wall sometimes. Yes. When? Where? Irene's place? Good! We can even go to Mosoja's joint. You know I love these two shebeens, they've got a touch of class ... yes for people like us. That's why all the visiting superstars are taken there for entertainment ... the Champion Jack Duprees, the Millie Jacksons and some football team directors enjoy themselves there. Even well known playwrights like the Maishe Maponyas and the Matsemela Manakas also go there for entertainment. Can't we fall under the same class? Good! you are a darling, what do you think I love you for? (*A bit disappointed*) C'ammon Joey you must pick me up. Please Joey fetch me, fetch me Joey? (*Excited again*) I knew you were joking. Now tell me, which car will you be driving? My favourite one? The red Colt Gallant? I love that one ... Love? I must go now to that boring job you know — come give me a kiss — mba! Mncpwa! (*Drops the phone and still excited*) Just imagine, Masonja's joint! Let's go dancing oolalaaah! (*She dances a bit and she freezes with her back to the audience.*)

MAGOGO: Haaibo! This can't be. Does this suggest that I must queue again just to pay? Why didn't that man take the money the same time he gave me the file?

Q. MARSHALL: Hey salukazi! You wake up and stop complaining! U ya kompleya, kompleya! Ag man! [You are complaining, complaining!]

(*NYAMEZO plays another nurse.*)

THIRD NURSE (*to another patient*): Yebo buti can I help you? O you want to go to Ward Fourteen. No problem, I can help you. You don't need enquiries. You go straight turn to your right, you will see red footmarks and they'll lead you to Ward Fourteen … Tell me are you sick? I mean with a tie and a suit on, you don't look sick to me. What? This necklace? My grandmother gave it to me (*giggle*). Who me? Thank you, thank you! (*giggle*) I live in Soweto — Chiawela. I work in this ward. Yes you can visit me at anytime … Just follow my directions and you won't get lost. Okay, bye-bye. Hope to see you again! (*freezes*)

MAGOGO (*to audience*): After another hour. I was told to go to the nurse. I tried to protest. A ngizanga ku nesi apha, ngifuna udokotela! I've not come to the nurse, I want the Doctor.

Q. MARSHALL: Salukazi are you still here? Awu guli wena mos! You are not sick! Uzo cheka la! You've come for your boyfriends! Fuck off! (*Exit* **Q. MARSHALL**)

MAGOGO (*to audience*): I lost the battle and I queued.

Nyamezo plays herself and attends to **MAGOGO**. *A BLACK DOCTOR played by* **FEZILE** *comes in.*

NYAMEZO (*after looking at* **MAGOGO**'s *file*): I'm sorry, Gogo, I can't handle your case. I will refer you to the doctor.

MAGOGO (*exploding*): I told you I wanted to see a doctor!

NYAMEZO Gogo this is the procedure here …

MAGOGO: Rubbish procedure! It's procedure! Procedure! Everywhere you go. Orderless procedure. (*To audience*) I was now running mad.

BLACK DOCTOR (*to* **MAGOGO**): Next please. (*Remembers*) Ah it's you again Gogo? And what's wrong this time? Pain? Let's see your card. All right I will prescribe some very good medicine for you. Good. You must go to the chemist and collect your medicine, but make sure that you come back here next Monday.

MAGOGO: Doctor you mean I must go and queue again here?

B. DOCTOR: No Gogo. This time of day there are not a lot of patients around here. (*She moves out*) No Gogo the chemist is on your right. Next please!

The **BLACK DOCTOR** *holds the 'chemist' board and freezes whilst* **MAGOGO** *comes to the counter for her medication. A WHITE* **PHARMACIST** *appears behind the counter.*

PHARMACIST: Come Magogo, let's see. (*Scrutinises the card*) No, no Magogo, go back to your doctor for motivation!

MAGOGO (*confused*):   Usukhuluma ngani manje, mntanami? [What are you talking about now, my child?]

PHARMACIST: I said motivation, motivation, Magogo!

(*She goes to* **NYAMEZO** *for help*)

MAGOGO: Angiyitholanga imithi futhi angiyizwa nale ndoda ekhuluma ngokungishawuda; wozongisiza ntombazana yami. [I didn't get the medicine, also I can't understand this man who shouts at me. Come and help me my girl.]

NYAMEZO *takes her to the chemist.*

PHARMACIST (*to Nurse*):   I told her to go for motivation! Motivation, Magogo!

NYAMEZO: But Doctor, I can't understand this. This is the third patient you have sent back for motivation ...

PHARMACIST: And the first two were changed. What's wrong in changing the prescription for this one?

NYAMEZO: Yes, but what I don't understand is that the doctor has actually examined the patient and has prescribed exactly what he knows will cure the patient.

PHARMACIST: I don't dispute that when the patient is young. The old people just waste medicine — they don't take it regularly. Hypertension tablets are very expensive, sister — and you know there is a very low compliance. The follow up on patients is poor, so why waste expensive medicine? Next please!

(*song, led by* **NYAMEZO**)

Wozani Manesi	Come nurses
Wezw'e simnyama	Of the black nation
Wozani silweni lomkhuba	Come let's fight these strange
Nxo — Nxo — Nxo	goings on
Kwaf'a bantwana	Children die

Imith'ikhona | While medication is there
Wozani silweni lomkhumba | Come let's fight these strange
Nxo — Nxo — Nxo | goings on

NYAMEZO (*to audience*): A few months later I was called to the local hospital security where I was told that …

LOC. SECURITY: Nyamezo, you are organising misconduct amongst the nurses! You are stirring them up! Your behaviour is intolerable and unprofessional. You will be dealt with severely …

NYAMEZO (*to audience*): And then came the Security Branch to: "take me for a drive". I was blindfolded and put at the back of the van. And during the 'honeymoon' with the Security Branch I was told in no uncertain terms that …

TRANSITION. The two male actors put on the white masks and march to confront **NYAMEZO**. *They stand on either side of her, and sing.*

SECURITY BRANCH: We will panel beat you kaffir
We will panel beat you goed.
Take you to Protea station
Panel beat you
Take you to Modderbee
Leave you naked
Take you to John Vorster Square
Los jou morsdood …
We will panelbeat you kaffir
We will panelbeat you goed.

NYAMEZO: I was told to bring the Health Workers Association constitution which I promised to bring, for I have seen cars being panel-beaten. But when I realised I was being turned into an informer, I discussed it with my husband. He was angry with me for offering to assist the police.

CHORUS: In state security!

NYAMEZO: So I never complied. Instead I became brave. We cannot go into battle when we do not expect casualties …

A continuation of the song 'Wozani manesi'

Hey wena vuka	Hey you wake up
Wesaba bani	Who do you fear
Vukani silweni lomkhuba …	Wake up let's fight these strange
Nxo — nxo — nxo	goings on …

SCENE EIGHT

A gathering of the South African Nursing Association (SANA) members. A white official is making some points. NYAMEZO is present. Only the last bits of her speech can be heard.

OFFICIAL: … The South African Nursing Association needs your full support. To bring this body closer to you we will take another look at the constitution to change it. So far we are very happy with the way things have gone. Our critics have also acknowledged this point. And for this reason we must give ourselves a standing ovation! (*Some of the other nurses give the speaker a standing ovation. NYAMEZO starts ululating and addresses the audience. The other nurses take seats.*)

NYAMEZO: Liiiiiiwu! liiiiwu! Ngcanda Kwedini agcwal'amancgwaba Umongikazi ebhekile! Ngcanda kwedini agcwal' amancgwaba Umongikazi ebhekile! Mongikazi wase Afrika! Have you forgotten the day you took your vow? Did you vow to let your people die in front of you? Or are you scared to follow your convictions? Two patients in a bed for one! Overcrowding! And where do our children get malnutrition in a rich country like ours? No! no! That's nonsense! That's nonsense! We must form our own union. Nurses of Afrika, you are the light you are the life, you are the light you are the life, you are the light you are the life! Mongikazi omnyama ongubozimhlophe! Floors, floors are beds for dying millions of your people! Au wena Owavela nokukhanya Kwelanga! There is life in your hands, resuscitate them to life because you can! It is inevitable that we must now form our own union! The situation here is being reinforced and aggravated by the poorly-qualified so-called doctors — the Taiwanese, the Polish, the Israelis, the Germans and all those chance-takers who could not make it in their countries. This is their Canaan. There is manna here for them. Yes, the authoritian type of institution is showing its true colours ...

A MALE NURSE raises his hand. He gets the approval of the meeting to speak.

FIRST MALE NURSE: To add to that ... recently a great number of qualified nurses have been refused permission to practise in the cities. The reason is that it is alleged that they come from the homelands. Ridiculous that this is done at a hospital level!

SECOND MALE NURSE (*interrupting*): Who cares where a nurse comes from?

FIRST MALE NURSE: Now, what I fail to understand is that the hospital also practises influx control! I agree to the formation of a union of the nurses, the doctors, the porters, and all other people who are employed in the hospitals. We are a trade! The hospital is a factory where broken bodies are being mended, you know! Yes, I support the formation of a union!

Applause. SECOND MALE NURSE stands up.

SECOND MALE NURSE: Sister Nyamezo, since we are all off-duty, I move that we take off these hospital uniforms so that we are not caught off-guard by the 'codes of conduct'.

All-out excitement as everybody starts to undress. Pandemonium. They sing.

Ndithi nyuka nxai ndini   [I say rise up you lazy ones
Ndithi nyuka nxai ndini   I say rise up you lazy ones
Ndithi nyuka nxai ndini   I say rise up you lazy ones!]

END

THE NUN'S
ROMANTIC STORY

A play by

Zakes Mda

THE NUN'S ROMANTIC STORY was first performed at the Civic Theatre, Johannesburg, on 23 March 1995, with the following cast of characters:

Sister Anna-Maria	—	Yael Farber
Father Villa	—	Jurgen Hellberg
Lawrence Pampiri	—	Sabata Sesiu
A.C. Malibu	—	Ernest Ndlovu
Senior Counsel	—	Iain Winter Smith

Directed by Jerry Mofokeng
Music by Tu Nokwe

Awarded the Olive Schreiner Prize for Drama, 1996, by the English Academy of Southern Africa.

(To apply for rights to perform this play contact:
DALRO, P O Box 31627, Braamfontein 2017, South Africa.)

THE NUN'S ROMANTIC STORY

CHARACTERS

ANNA-MARIA: A 29 year old nun, who teaches mathematics at a Catholic high school. Very beautiful. Must be able to play guitar. Not just play, but be real good at it.

LAWRENCE PAMPIRI: Geography teacher at the Catholic high school. Perhaps late thirties or early forties. Must be able to play flute. All the better if he is good at it too.

ATTORNEY A.C. MALIBU: Middle-aged local lawyer.

SENIOR COUNSEL: An elderly lawyer from abroad. Once professor and army general. Nobody will blame you if you think he tends to be judge and prosecutor at the same time. If at all you want him to be British, then he is Queen's Counsel.

FATHER VILLA: An elderly priest-in-charge at Our Lady of Fatima Cathedral. Saintly.

Four Girls: In their mid-teens. Students at the Catholic high school. All they do is sing really. Some miserly producer/director might decide to do without them, and let poor Anna-Maria sing alone and role-play their action.

SCENE 1

There are three distinct acting spaces on the stage, each representing a different place and/or a different time in the history of our characters. On the First Space is an austere bench, and on the Second Space two chairs. Throughout the play there are no other sets. When the play opens there is a pool of light on each of the two acting spaces. The Third Space is in darkness. Sister Anna-Maria sits on the First Space bench. She is a nun in a nun's habit. She is a very beautiful young woman of about twenty-nine. A guitar lies on the floor next to her bench. Lawrence Pampiri sits on one of the Second Space chairs, and is writing on a notebook. He is a teacher in his late thirties or early forties.

ANNA-MARIA (*laughingly*): The ribs of the devil. That's what the early missionaries called the guitar. They would never have allowed a Christian to have anything to do with it. How things have changed. Today we play it in church. Guitar, drums, handclapping ... during High Mass.

(*Pampiri stops writing, and looks up at the audience*)

PAMPIRI: Often she brought me cookies from the convent. I would open my cupboard in the staff-room and there would be cookies, nicely wrapped in a powder-blue tissue paper. Cookies with raisins in them.

(*Anna-Maria takes her guitar and plays a few bars. She smiles and puts it down again.*)

ANNA-MARIA: I am glad that they finally agreed that I could have my guitar with me here. I don't know how Father Villa managed to persuade them, but I am so glad he was able to.

PAMPIRI: Sometimes there would be cookies and red wine. Just half a bottle of wine. It was wine which remained when she was preparing the altar for the Communion service. It always tasted flat, but since it was from her it was alright.

ANNA-MARIA: Imagine! They were saying I might use it to commit suicide. Perhaps cut my wrists with the strings, or tie the strings around my throat until I could not breathe anymore. Desecrate an instrument that can produce such beautiful sounds. How crude can you get! If that is their fear, they might just as well leave me naked. I might hang myself with my knickers.

PAMPIRI: It was done so furtively that none of the other teachers noticed. We all went about our day-to-day business of teaching our students, and the globe continued to rotate on its axis. You know, I don't care much for sweet things. Always have been a savoury person. But then I enjoyed the intrigue.

(*He goes back to his writing, and she strums the guitar. Only a few haunting bars. Lights dim to black.*)

SCENE 2

Lights rise on the Second Space. Senior Counsel and Attorney A.C. Malibu are sitting on the two chairs, facing each other. Although Senior Counsel, or S.C., is in fact an advocate or barrister from abroad he is dressed in a judge's robe, and wears a judge's wig. Under his robe we can clearly see his military uniform with many medals. Otherwise he is a sanguine elderly gentleman with a grey head and a friendly face. A.C. Malibu is much younger, and has an air about him of a man who takes himself quite seriously. He is reading from a sheaf of papers. The other two acting spaces are in darkness.

MALIBU (*reading*): "Soldiers from the capital city had marched in the morning, and every pathway in the village was full of strangers with guns."

(*He suddenly stands up agitated, and paces the floor.*)

There was a good reason, Prof. I tell you there was a good reason.

S.C.: There is always a good reason, A.C. You do not have to bear the guilt ... or to justify things that happened many years ago. Otherwise you are bearing the guilt for other people.

MALIBU: Twenty years ago when we refused to hand over power to the opposition party after they had won the elections, it was to save this country from communism.

S.C.: Come back, A.C. Sit down, and let's hear what more she has to say for herself.

(*A.C. Malibu sits on his chair.*)

MALIBU (*reading*): "No one knew exactly what they wanted, but everyone knew that immediately after the elections the government had declared a state of emergency throughout the country."

S.C.: You had lost the elections, so you declared a state of emergency instead of handing over power to the party that had won.

MALIBU: We had wanted to hand over. I was the President's

legal adviser at the time. He was quite willing to hand over, but was advised against it.

S.C.: You advised him against it then?

MALIBU: You cannot put your guilt on me, Prof. You did. I, as the President's adviser, merely advised him to take your advice.

S.C.: So I did, did I? Of course. Forgive me, old chap, for the lapse of memory. You see, I have had a lot of adventures in the international political theatre. You understand, of course, that the advice I gave at the time was given in good faith on behalf of my principals, namely West Germany, the United Kingdom and the United States. We felt very strongly at the time that the opposition party was under the influence of the eastern bloc. It was before perestroika. Before glasnost. The chills of the cold war were sweeping the world, and it was crucial for us, western democracies, to maintain our spheres of influence in the developing world.

MALIBU: It didn't matter that the opposition had won a democratic election ...

S.C.: Well, we did espouse — and believe it or not, practise — democracy in our countries, but in the Third World we were quite prepared to subvert democracy to safeguard our interests.

MALIBU: Often we ended up with a bunch of corrupt buffoons who were being propped up by the west.

S.C.: I was a military commander seconded to your armed forces at the time. The western governments instructed me to strongly urge your President not to hand over power. When he seemed to weaken I was quite prepared to shoot him.

MALIBU: Well, you can't blame him. We were amateurs at coups. We still had the notions of democracy that we were taught throughout our education existed in your country. I have a vivid memory of that. Twenty years! It's like yesterday. That was the first coup of its kind. We have had many after that. Our first coup. All the opposition party leaders were locked up, and we began a nationwide campaign against all prominent opposition supporters.

S.C.: There were atrocities.

MALIBU: Stories of atrocities were told from village to village, but the radio never reported these. Instead they played martial music throughout the day. And the next day, and next … It went on like that.

S.C.: You know, A.C. Malibu, I want to tell you that democracy lies in the eye of the beholder. Just like terrorism. My terrorist is your freedom fighter. When the United States mines the harbours of Nicaragua it is terrorism to you, but to me it is an act of protecting the freedom of the western hemisphere. Well, so much for that. It is neither here nor there at the moment. Continue with reading me the statement.

MALIBU (*reading*): "Soldiers were on the rampage in the village, pillaging and burning everything in front of them…"

Sudden light on the First and Third Spaces. Father Villa, an elderly Catholic priest in a saintly poise stands on the Third Space. The two lawyers were taken by surprise by the sudden lights. They look at him. Sister Anna-Maria quietly sits on her First Space bench, and will follow the following dialogue with interest.

VILLA: You will defend her, Mr A.C. Malibu. You promised you will.

MALIBU: I must admit that at first I was quite reluctant to defend her. I mean after what she did.

S.C.: Alleged to have done.

MALIBU: Well, we all know she did it. She says so herself.

S.C.: It's still an allegation.

MALIBU: That's just a legal nicety, of course.

VILLA: The church is quite prepared to support her at all costs.

MALIBU: That is why I agreed, Father, to take this case. Otherwise I would not have touched it with a ten foot pole. I mean I am an orthodox Catholic lawyer. There are many things that dismay us in this country now.

VILLA: We are just as dismayed with the direction this country is taking. When you refused to hand over power to the opposition we supported that to the hilt. It was also in the interests of the Catholic church to save this country from communism. We preached in our churches throughout this country against the opposition.

MALIBU: Indeed we are dismayed, Father. The very government that we saved can now be heard espousing leftist ideas. They even established diplomatic relations with communist countries.

S.C.: Don't worry, Father. She will be defended.

MALIBU: Yes. That's why I got him. (*pointing at S.C.*) He is a Senior Counsel from abroad. He will handle this case very brilliantly.

VILLA: I am sure he will.

MALIBU: He was my professor at the university when I studied law. That's why I call him Prof. I have all the confidence in him.

VILLA: She does not seem to understand the gravity of her actions. She is innocent.

Anna-Maria suddenly stands up, and for the first time she is angry. Only briefly though, for the anger melts into a smile. Her smile is not a mechanical one that is only on her lips. It is in her eyes as well, in her face and in her voice.

ANNA-MARIA: No! I am not innocent. It is an utter insult to refer to me in those terms. I cannot be innocent. I refuse to be innocent. And if anyone of you wants to order that I be granted freedom, I will resist with all my might.

The lawyers are astounded. Father Villa gives her a saintly reassuring smile. Lights gradually go down on First and Second Spaces until black.

S.C.: What I want to know is, was her action a political statement?

MALIBU: I don't understand, Prof.

S.C.: Was this a political act, or was she driven by other passions? Are we at one stage going to be required to

advance political arguments in our defence? In short, are
we characters in a political play?

MALIBU: Our defence is obsession.

S.C.: Obsession? What kind of defence is that? Insanity. That's
the only defence I can see here.

MALIBU: Obsession!

Lights fall to black.

SCENE 3

*Lights rise on all the three spaces. Sister Anna-Maria stands on her
bench on the First Space. Father Villa is on the Third Space. They
directly face the audience. On the Second Space stands Senior
Counsel, also facing the audience. Throughout this scene they
remain in this position, addressing the dialogue directly to the particular spot they are fixedly looking. Anna-Maria, though, will later
sit down and play her guitar.*

S.C.: You understand that you are under oath?

ANNA-MARIA (*raises her hand*): So help me God.

S.C.: You were nine years old at the time?

ANNA-MARIA: Yes, my Lord.

S.C.: And you were a very happy little girl.

ANNA-MARIA: I am still very happy.

S.C.: You want to be happy, Anna-Maria, but you cannot be
happy. Circumstances do not allow you to be happy.

ANNA-MARIA: They have decreed that I should not be happy,
but I decided to defy that. I am happy your Lordship. No
argument in the world will convince me that I am not.

S.C.: We digress again. We must keep to the point, Anna-
Maria. We do not want irrelevancies to cloud our evidence. It was in the evening, you say, and you were sitting
at table having supper?

ANNA-MARIA (*smiles*): It was my father, and my mother,
and my little brother, and myself. We were having supper,
yes.

S.C.: How old was your brother?

ANNA-MARIA: He was five years old.

S.C.: And your father was the village school teacher.

ANNA-MARIA: Yes, my Lord, he taught at the local primary school.

S.C.: Then what happened. Anna-Maria?

ANNA-MARIA: In fact he was the principal there.

S.C.: What happened that evening, Anna-Maria?

ANNA-MARIA: I am tired. She says I must sit down and answer no more questions.

S.C.: Who says?

ANNA-MARIA: I cannot tell you. You won't understand.

S.C.: Well, you cannot sit down. You are giving evidence. In a court of law. Under oath.

ANNA-MARIA: I will sit down all the same. You can continue the trial without me.

(*She sits on the bench and softly plays her guitar.*)

S.C. (*exasperated*): The evidence, Anna-Maria! The evidence!

VILLA: Then they heard the ominous sound of marching boots outside. And the crazy laughter of drunken soldiers.

S.C.: But you cannot give evidence on her behalf, Father Villa.

VILLA: The soldiers kicked the door open. They never knocked. They kicked the door open and walked into the room. No questions. Nothing. They lined the family against the wall. And they ate all the food in the house.

S.C.: Please, Father Villa.

VILLA: After the feast, the school teacher and the two little children were forced, at gun point, to watch as the soldiers took turns to rape the woman of the home. He tried to struggle to save his wife, but he was handcuffed, and thoroughly beaten. This agony lasted for hours, the man a powerless spectator, and the children screaming. At first the woman screamed too, but a few vicious blows on the jaw with the butt of the gun saw to it that she shut up. Anyway she could only produce a gurgling sound since her mouth was full of blood. In the early hours of the morning the soldiers were tired of their game. The commander ordered that the whole family be shot, and of course the soldiers derived much fun in spreading volleys of bullets across the room. Bodies fell. The soldiers marched out, singing a triumphant song.

S.C.: Oh, my God, what have we done!

VILLA: By some miracle of the Holy Ghost, Anna-Maria survived — was only grazed in the arm. Everyone in the family instantly died, but Anna-Maria was saved. She ran to the nearest place where she hoped she would get sanctuary, the Catholic mission station not far from her home. The nuns took her in.

Lights fall to dark. The last strains of Anna-Maria's guitar can be heard in the dark.

SCENE 4

Lights rise on the Second Space. Attorney Malibu and S.C. sit on the two chairs, facing each other.

S.C.:   I don't believe in your defence. Too dramatic. I mean, too histrionic. It is the kind of defence that you would read in a Morris West novel.

MALIBU: This is for real, Prof, and we can make it work for us.

S.C.: Obsession?

MALIBU: Obsession. It can work. You see, Prof, you taught me to dare ... to look for the unusual in a case.

S.C.:   I don't know. This is so far-fetched ... it has no legal basis. But then if you explain to me how you hope it will work ... The whole family was killed ...

MALIBU: The whole family, except Anna-Marie. The next morning the school teacher's house was a heap of smouldering ruins, for the soldiers set the house on fire before they left.

S.C.:   We have two miracles here. First Anna-Maria escapes the bullets, and then the fire.

MALIBU: The villagers tried to rummage through the rubble, but nothing could be saved. It was the same case with all the other places that were burnt down by the soldiers the previous night.

S.C.: I know that we sent the soldiers out to crush the opposition. What I don't understand, A.C., were these rampaging soldiers raping and burning places at random? How did they choose the target houses?

MALIBU: Whole families of known opposition supporters were wiped out. It is said that ruling party members supplied the soldiers with lists of potential victims, and accompanied the soldiers to point out the targeted houses.

S.C. (*shocked*): My God! These people! The untold cruelty they are capable of ... on their own people too!

MALIBU (*angry*): Okay, blame it on my people then. They are savage, eh, barbaric ... You forget that you are the source of all these problems. The neo-colonial powers created all this present mess.

S.C. That's right. Blame it on colonialism. I know that syndrome very well. I have seen it a lot of times throughout the Third World. When you have been circus buffoons who murdered and ate school children, and you have then crowned yourselves with an imperial crown of gold at the market square for all the world to see and laugh, you have blamed it on colonialism.

MALIBU: In this instance, Prof, you were the Supreme Commander of our armed forces, seconded by your government to teach us how to be good soldiers. When these things happened you were in the middle of it all.

S.C.: But you did not see me go to the villages to pillage and rape your women. No one can say he ever saw my face there.

MALIBU: You planned the terror in the safety of your office.

S.C.: If it was not good for them, the soldiers would have defied my orders. They had fun. Let alone profit from the property that they looted. Your soldiers and their commanders were not just puppets in my hands. We were partners. And indeed I always made a point of establishing democratic structures among the senior officers.

MALIBU: Well, Prof, it does not do us any good to apportion blame now. After all we were all involved in this. You ordered us to stage a coup, and we followed your orders. We could have defied your orders if we did not think a coup was good for us.

S.C.:   All I am saying is that I will not accept blame for this. It was for a great cause. People who died sacrificed their lives for freedom, and for the survival of western civilization in these dark parts of the world.

MALIBU: Look, Prof …

S.C.:   After all it is all in the past. Now the world is a different place. The Soviet might has been crushed. The evil empire is no more, so there is no more competition for spheres of influence in the developing world. You can no longer play one super power against the other in order to get maximum benefits from aid packages. The whole world now is in the palm of our hand. Our super attention is elsewhere. We are busy exploiting new markets than to worry about your petty little selves. You can now happily boil in your own soup.

By now he is very excited, and is ludicrously dancing around.

MALIBU (*shaking him*):   Goddamnit Professor! What has this got to do with the defence that we need to formulate?

S.C.:   Sorry, old chap. I get carried away sometimes. Back to the defence, eh? Let us hear more of the facts.

MALIBU: The villagers were pleased to hear that at least one member of the school teacher's family escaped death, and was safe at the mission station.

S.C.:   In an earlier statement it was revealed that there was no love lost between the mission station and a large segment of the village community.

MALIBU: Village politics. Indeed the villagers were quite surprised that the nuns gave the little girl sanctuary. It was a well-known fact that the school teacher had been at loggerheads with the Catholic church on many issues. The church regarded him as a communist since he belonged to the opposition party.

S.C.: Well, it is a fact that the Catholic church openly supported your ruling party.

MALIBU: Whereas the Protestant churches were more in line with the opposition party. The villagers, of course, were active participants in this hot mixture of state and church politics. Hadn't the Catholic priest preached in church the Sunday before the election that people should not vote for the opposition party since they were communists? Everyone knew that communists were anti-Christ.

S.C.: That I remember very well. The President was so sure of victory because the Catholics form a vast majority of the people in your country here.

MALIBU: Yes. We were quite so rudely shocked when we lost. And of course you came along and advised us not to hand over power.

S.C.: So Anna-Maria was brought up by the nuns from the age of nine and has lived with them ever since.

MALIBU: That is as far as I got, Prof. Most of the information comes from Father Villa, or from Sister Mary-Ellen, the American nun who is the principal of the high school. And of course there is Lawrence Pampiri the high school teacher. He is a very important witness. As a matter of fact they want to make him state witness. It is very difficult to get information from Anna-Maria.

S.C.: But she is our most crucial source of information!

MALIBU: She changes, Prof. She's got all types of different moods. Sometimes she cooperates and answers our questions. Then all of a sudden she changes and won't answer anymore.

S.C.: Why is she so difficult? Doesn't she realize that we want to save her?

MALIBU (*reverently*): She says she gets her instructions from ' the Virgin Mary. She hears the Virgin's voice.

S.C.: Oh, come on now, A.C.!

MALIBU: True, Prof. Sometimes the Blessed Virgin tells her not to say a word. Then all she does is sit down and play her guitar.

S.C.: Oh, no! Who the hell does she think she is? Some kind of Joan of Arc or Agnes of God?

MALIBU (*even more reverently*): She says the virgin will send her angels to rescue her. She will fly with them through the barred window then through the clouds into heaven.

S.C. (*laughs so much that tears roll down his cheek*): You don't believe in all this hocus-pocus about flying virgins, do you, old chap?

MALIBU (*embarrassed*): Well, Prof, all I can say is that miracles have been known to happen.

S.C. (*still laughing*): For the judges of this world, of course, we must prepare our defence, in the temporal manner that things are done this side of heaven. Perhaps this will even strengthen our case. Clearly the woman is insane!

Lights fall to black

SCENE 5

Lights rise on each of the three spaces. Sister Anna-Maria sits on her bench on the First Space, softly playing her guitar. The two lawyers are sitting on the chairs on the Second Space. The Third Space is bare

MALIBU: She was obsessed with the idea of vengeance from the age of nine. She never grew up. She is still a nine year old girl.

S.C.: What is your evidence for that?

MALIBU: You heard what the principal of the high school said.

S.C.: The American nun … eh …

MALIBU: Sister Mary-Ellen. And also Lawrence Pampiri's evidence. Often she was seen frolicking with school girls, playing their silly games.

Four giggling school girls in their mid-teens enter Third Space.

They are in school uniform, and they chase one another around with noise and carefree laughter. Their glee attracts Anna-Maria's attention, and she stops playing the guitar. Taking it with her, she friskily runs to join them. The two lawyers watch all this with great interest. From now to the end of the scene they will be silent spectators. In fact, so that they must not attract too much of the audience's attention, the light on their space falls a bit, and is more on the dim side. This also applies to the light on the deserted First Space. These two spaces must however not be in total darkness, for we want to be constantly aware of them. In fact the audience must clearly see the bench and the two lawyers. They must be aware of the lawyers' reaction to the events of this scene. It might not be amiss to have a bright yellowish light which gives a dreamlike effect of the Third Space.

GIRL 1: Let us play a game of rounders.

GIRL 2: The bell will ring before we complete the game. Let's play follow-your-leader instead.

GIRL 3: And why should we play what you want us to play?

GIRL 4: Maybe we should just sit down and talk about boys.

ANNA-MARIA: I'll tell you what, let us sing and dance instead.

They hold hands and dance around in a circle, while singing. The song can be any innocently naughty song that is well-known in the area. It can be a bit saucy if you like, but not crude or explicit. After the dance they all sit down around Anna-Maria, who plays the guitar.

ALL (*singing*): He's got the whole world
In His hands
He's got the whole world
In His hands

He's got the fish of the sea
In His hands
He's got the birds of the air
In His hands
He's got the whole world
In His hands

He's got the gangling man
In His hands
He's got the sailor man
In His hands
He's got the whole world
In His hands

He's got the tiny little baby
In His hands
He's got the little bitsy baby
In His hands
He's got the whole world
In His hands

He's got everybody here
In His hands
He's got you and me sister
In His hands
He's got the whole world
In His hands

The bell rings.

ANNA-MARIA: Okay girls, break is over. Back to class.

The giggling school girls run away.

ANNA-MARIA (*shouting after them*): And don't forget our meeting of the Legion of Mary this afternoon!

She sits down and plays very complicated chords, and hums in her mellifluous voice. After a few moments Lawrence Pampiri enters and is immediately transfixed by the music. Anna-Maria plays for a while, and stops. She looks up at him and smiles.

PAMPIRI: Where did you learn to play like that?

ANNA-MARIA: Just by myself, on my own.

PAMPIRI: You mean nobody taught you?

ANNA-MARIA: I taught myself. I just play, you know. I don't even remember ever learning to play.

PAMPIRI: Amazing. I play the flute. We must get together and play sometime. Of course, I am not nearly as good as you are. But we can make a smashing duo.

ANNA-MARIA: All right.

PAMPIRI: You are the new mathematics teacher?

ANNA-MARIA: Well, not that new. I have been here for six months now.

PAMPIRI: I guess you are right. Six months can be a long time, especially with the type of students we have. I teach here too. Been teaching here for the last seven years.

ANNA-MARIA: I haven't seen you in the staffroom before.

PAMPIRI: I was away when you came, on study leave. Just came back.

ANNA-MARIA: A flute sounds very nice. Maybe we should play in church one of these Sundays.

PAMPIRI: I don't go to church.

ANNA-MARIA: Why?

PAMPIRI: I am an atheist.

ANNA-MARIA: What religion is that?

PAMPIRI: It's no religion. I don't believe in the existence of God.

ANNA-MARIA: You must be joking, of course. Everybody believes in the existence of God.

PAMPIRI: I am serious.

ANNA-MARIA: Then how come you teach here, in a Catholic school?

PAMPIRI: This is a good school, and I am a good teacher. So I teach here. I don't teach religion.

ANNA-MARIA (*obviously she finds this intriguing*): Does Sister Mary-Ellen know? I am sure she does not. Don't worry, I won't tell on you.

PAMPIRI (*amused*): She knows very well. We talk about it sometimes. She is very broadminded, you know. She herself is a socialist, and believes in liberation theology. Got converted into liberation theology when she worked in Nicaragua.

ANNA-MARIA: I wouldn't keep you here if I were principal.

PAMPIRI: That's what Father Villa thinks. You have met Father Villa who is in charge of Our Lady of Fatima

Cathedral. He thinks I should have been long kicked out of this school. After a thorough flogging, of course. Although Mary-Ellen is appalled at my beliefs, she firmly believes that as a progressive within the Catholic church she shouldn't concern herself with the religious beliefs of her staff, as long as they don't spread such beliefs to the students.

ANNA-MARIA: My God! I have never heard anything of the sort. You seem so sensible, yet you say such stupid things.

PAMPIRI: You seem like a sensible girl yourself. And beautiful. How come you are a nun?

ANNA-MARIA (*rather flattered*): Beautiful sensible girls become nuns.

PAMPIRI: That's a wasted beauty. Maybe you should marry me, and we shall live happily ever after.

ANNA-MARIA: I am married to Jesus.

PAMPIRI (*laughs*):   And your mother-in-law is Mary, who happens to be a virgin.

ANNA-MARIA (*not offended at all*): You think it's funny, don't you?

PAMPIRI: All religion is comedy. But you haven't told me how you became a nun.

ANNA-MARIA: At a very early age the Virgin Mary mapped out my path. From the age of nine I lived in the convent with the nuns, while I attended the village mission school.

PAMPIRI: Your parents gave over to a convent?

ANNA-MARIA: My parents were killed during the State of Emergency. So I went to live with the nuns. Some of my close relatives tried to take me away from the convent, but I refused. I was much happier there. I learnt my lessons well, and was later sent to a boarding school. After completing high school, I took my vows and became a nun. Then I went to university, graduated with honours in mathematics, and here I am now teaching at this high school, and relating my life history to an atheist.

They both laugh. Lights fall to black on all the spaces.

SCENE 6

Lights rise on Father Villa on the Third Space. He addresses the audience.

VILLA: They have often asked me, "Why Father? Why do you believe so strongly in her innocence? After all everyone saw her do it." How can I explain this? How can I tell them that what they saw is not really what they thought they saw? You might not understand this, but I think God used her hand to save this country. I may even go as far as to say she is incapable of sin. And how do I know this? A priest, anointed as a disciple of Christ, always knows. After all it is the priests of this world who determine who goes to heaven or not. They decide who should go through all the process from beatification to canonization. We officially decide who God should accept into His Kingdom as saints, and therefore God's own counsellors. I do not see why my declaration on Anna-Maria should amaze anybody, when saints are created by us here on earth.

We saw a relationship of sorts develop between Anna-Maria and Lawrence Pampiri, and we all frowned upon it. Oh, yes. Even Mary-Ellen frowned upon it. The difference between the two of us was that whereas I have always wanted to take action against it, Mary-Ellen was ruled by the strange American notion of respecting other people's privacy. I tried to drum it into her head that Anna-Maria was a child of God, and therefore could not possibly have any privacy. I do not want you to get me wrong. I am not suggesting anything immoral in the relationship. There is no doubt in our mind that the relationship between the two was a platonic one. Anna-Maria was not capable of sin, although Pampiri himself was a scoundrel who would have long been kicked out of the school were it not for the liberal American nun. God knows I spoke with her a number of times. I mean with Mary-Ellen. She fiercely dismissed me since she believed that I was interfering in the affairs of the high school, which was her sole jurisdiction as principal. I was in charge of Our Lady of Fatima Cathedral, and had no business in the high school, she said.

I have heard the lawyers talk about Anna-Maria's state of mind. There is nothing wrong with her state of mind. She frolicked with little girls, not because of any immaturity on her part, but because like all saints she loved children. I know that the older sisters, the more conservative ones, sometimes thought she went too far in her interaction with the girls. But they loved her all the same. Some of them treated her like a little girl who needed guidance herself.

From all this you can see that our views differed considerably on Anna-Maria. But one thing we all agreed about: we all loved her.

Lights fade to black.

SCENE 7

Lights rise on Anna-Maria on the First Space, and Pampiri on the Second Space. Pampiri has his flute with him.

PAMPIRI (*to the audience*):   I don't know how to tell you this ... I mean in a way that you won't misinterpret it, but a special friendship developed between Sister Anna-Maria and myself. A very special relationship. Okay, let me admit it at once, I was falling hopelessly in love with her. I have never mentioned this to anyone, for it shames me. There is no point in hiding it now, for you are bound to find out about it at the trial. You see, I am going to give evidence, under oath, and there is no way I'll be able to hide this. It might as well come out now.

ANNA-MARIA (*addressing the audience*): "Your father was a communist," that's what the sisters at the village mission station used to tell me. "But we pray for his soul everyday. May it rest in peace." They told me this everyday. Until I believed that there was something terribly wrong that my father had done, and therefore he deserved to die.

PAMPIRI: I have given the matter much thought since then, and I have come to the conclusion that the passion that I had for Anna-Maria was of a physical nature. I wanted, more than anything else, to uncover and explore the mysteries that were hidden under her habit. Perhaps I was not even hopelessly in love with her. It was the question of the mysteries. And the haunting music. On the other hand it is quite possible I was hopelessly in love with her. I don't know. All I know is that from then on every woman I slept with I would change into Anna-Maria by the sheer force of my imagination.

ANNA-MARIA: When I was a kid I had nightmares. Well, personally I don't remember any of that. But Mother Superior told me that I used to have nightmares. I outgrew that, though.

PAMPIRI: I was free with her. We were both free. So I told her how I felt about her, and my secret desires and fantasies. She laughed. She always laughed at everything.

ANNA-MARIA (*rattling on like a school girl reciting what she has learnt by heart*):   Did you know that although this is called a Spanish guitar it actually originates in Egypt and was introduced to Spain by Arabs? Now, many people dispute that. They say that there is no trace among the instruments of the Arabs known to us of any instrument similar to the guitar in construction and shape. Although the guitar was at one time strung in unison-pairs like the lute, it is now commonly provided with six single-strings tuned in fourths, except between the second and third strings where the interval is a major third. The lowest string is E below the bass stave, and the notation is an octave above the actual sounds. Chords and arpeggios are characteristic of its technique which make it well suited for accompanying singers. (*She laughs*) I read that in an encyclopaedia. I don't know what it really means. I just play the guitar.

PAMPIRI: To her everything was a joke. That's one other thing that made her so attractive. She had the gift of laughter. The kind of laughter that sent tingles of pleasure down your spine. She did not take herself, nor the world, seriously. Take the question of my atheism.

As he walks to the Third Space, lights fall to black on the Second Space. Anna-Maria has seen him walk to the Third Space, so she also takes her guitar, and goes on to join him there. Lights fall to black on the space she has left as well.

PAMPIRI: I enjoyed the cookies. Thanks.

ANNA-MARIA (*laughs*):   What cookies?

PAMPIRI: The cookies that you put in my cupboard in the staffroom.

ANNA-MARIA: How did you know I put them there?

PAMPIRI: It's like a valentine card. It will be anonymous, but you will always know where it came from.

ANNA-MARIA: I don't know anything about valentine cards.

PAMPIRI: Well, the cookies had an air of sanctity about them. I knew at once they were from the convent.

ANNA-MARIA: What would an atheist know about sanctity?

PAMPIRI: As a matter of fact …

ANNA-MARIA: How did you become an atheist?

PAMPIRI: What?

ANNA-MARIA: You heard me. How did you become an atheist? I told you how I became a nun, you didn't tell me how you became an atheist.

PAMPIRI: So it's a question of you show me yours I'll show you mine.

ANNA-MARIA: You show me your what?

PAMPIRI: Forget it. I became an atheist at high school.

ANNA-MARIA: What happened?

PAMPIRI: Although I was Catholic my parents sent me to a Protestant high school, because it was the best high school in the country at the time.

ANNA-MARIA: You mean Catholics who go to Protestant high schools become atheists?

PAMPIRI: Do not be in a hurry for the gravy before the meat is ready. You know, at high school we were forced to go to church. Very much as you do now to the students here at school. Every Sunday we had to go to church. And so I attended the Catholic church which was a few miles from my school.

ANNA-MARIA: That was good. You attended your own church. And so?

PAMPIRI: Remember what I told you about the meat and gravy?

ANNA-MARIA: I want you to get to the point.

PAMPIRI: I am getting there! I am getting there!

ANNA-MARIA (*laughing*): So get there, dammit, and stop beating about the bush.

PAMPIRI: What did you say?

ANNA-MARIA: Stop beating about ....

PAMPIRI: No, the other thing. "Dammit!" Nice girls, who are nuns to boot, don't use such language.

ANNA-MARIA: It is your bad influence. Fancy, teaching a nun to swear!

PAMPIRI: Anyway, one Sunday in church, the priest — Father Hamel was his name — suddenly stopped the sermon. He was looking at me. He whispered something to one of the catechists, pointing in my direction. The catechist came down to me and whispered in my ear, "Father Hamel says you must go out of his church at once!" I wanted to know why, but was told that I could not question the reverend father's decisions. So I refused to leave. The catechist went back to Father Hamel and whispered something in his ear. The mass grudgingly continued after that.

ANNA-MARIA: You have always been a stubborn one then?

PAMPIRI: Well, the mass was over, and Father Hamel flew out in a most unceremonious fashion. He was waiting for me outside the main door of the church as I walked out. In the presence of everyone he shouted at me, "How dare you refuse when I say you must leave my church?"

"Because I don't know why I must leave."

"What do you want here?"

"Same thing that everyone else wants. To pray so that I may go to heaven when I die."

"What does a communist know about heaven? I don't want to see you here, do you hear me?"

"I hear you loud and clear, but still you haven't told me why."

"I do not want to talk to you. In fact I am giving you an anathema!"

I was getting real angry, but I mockingly laughed at his face, and shouted, "And I am giving it back to you, man! I am giving you a thousand anathemas, you little twerp!"

They both laugh.

Everybody gasped in shock. For sure nothing could save me from hell then, as far as the spectators were concerned. It turned out that because I was wearing my green blazer which also has the school badge he knew at once that I was from the Protestant high school. Our school was well-known for being pro-opposition party, while the Catholic church was actively campaigning for the ruling party. And of course the elections, the very elections that changed your life, were just around the corner. People like Father Hamel were in the centre of all the mess.

ANNA-MARIA: My God! Those elections!

PAMPIRI: Those elections, my dear Sister Anna-Maria. The only post-independence elections we have ever had. And they ended in a coup. I did not argue further with Father Hamel. To tell you the truth I was quite happy that he had expelled me from the church. You know that students hate to go to church, so for me this was going to be a good excuse. The only thing I had to do as soon as I got back to the high school would be to report to the principal that I had been officially expelled from the church, so that he might tell his prefects not to bother me about church again. I thought Father Hamel was great, and had saved me from the agony of walking all those miles every Sunday morning. And thanks God there was no other Catholic church for miles and miles around.

ANNA-MARIA: What did the principal say?

PAMPIRI: It was a mistake to tell him. He was really mad at Father Hamel. We drove back to the church in his car. Father Hamel refused to see us. When the principal insisted that he wanted to talk with him, he shouted that we were trespassing in his church yard, and if we did not leave immediately he was going to set his dogs on us. We left. I felt quite happy with myself, for surely after all that there was nobody who would force me to church. Wasn't the principal himself my witness that my own church did not want to have anything to do with me? But my elation did not last long, for the principal broke the silence and said, "Well, my boy, you will have to go to the Anglican church. After all there is no real difference between your church and the Anglicans."

They both laugh.

ANNA-MARIA: Do you want to know what I think about all this?

PAMPIRI: Tell me.

ANNA-MARIA: I think you were wrong ...

PAMPIRI: I was wrong! Listen to this woman! I was wrong! I am sitting in church minding my own business, when the priest decides to pick on me, and you say I was wrong!

ANNA-MARIA: I say you were wrong to become an atheist just because of the activities of one person.

PAMPIRI: To tell you the truth when these things were happening I was already having my doubts about religion. Hamel merely reinforced my disgust with the activities of the church.

ANNA-MARIA: I thought so.

PAMPIRI: I got disillusioned with the church, and later with religion in general. The early seeds of atheism were planted in me by the prefaces of George Bernard Shaw, particularly the preface to his play *Androcles and the Lion*. This was a set-book at school. This preface sparked my interest in the subject.

ANNA-MARIA: I do not know anything about him.

PAMPIRI: I expect so. Don't worry. It is not important at all in your life.

ANNA-MARIA (*after a pause*):   Do you think the church was wrong to get involved in politics?

PAMPIRI: It is a difficult question, Anna-Maria. I do not know how to answer it.

ANNA-MARIA: Why is it a difficult question? I would have thought there is a straight forward answer to that. Either the church must involve itself in politics or it must not.

PAMPIRI: It is not as straightforward as all that. Here in our country we have seen the bitter results of the church's negative involvement in national politics. We are living examples of that. Your family was wiped out, and I became an atheist.

ANNA-MARIA: My family was not wiped out by the church.

PAMPIRI: Not directly, no.

ANNA-MARIA: You don't know the answer to that one, do you, Lawrence?

PAMPIRI: No, I don't. Church interference in politics really depends on which side of the fence you stand. In a country like South Africa, for instance, clergymen such as Tutu, Mkhatshwa, Chikane and many others — not forgetting Trevor Huddleston before them — have played a great role in the liberation struggle of that country. Sometimes when all voices had been silenced, political leaders were in jail or in exile, these men and women — we remember Sister Ncube, who was a nun like yourself — kept the fires of resistance burning at home. I am sure to the regime of that country these church people were interfering in politics, whereas to the oppressed majority they were regarded as freedom fighters. In Latin America the church has played both roles, at different times, or different segments of the church ...

ANNA-MARIA: Both roles?

PAMPIRI: Both oppressor and liberator.

ANNA-MARIA: You know what, Lawrence, I think my greatest task now is to convince you back to the church. To wrestle for your soul with the devil, so to speak.

PAMPIRI: It will be my greatest pleasure to be reconverted by a beautiful woman like you.

ANNA-MARIA: I see you have brought your flute. Let us play.
She plays the guitar, and he joins in with his flute. They play on for some time. Lights fade to black. Music also fades out after some time.

SCENE 8

Lights rise on Anna-Maria on the First Space. She is standing on the bench. Her guitar is on the floor. At the same time lights rise on the two lawyers on the Second Space.

ANNA-MARIA (*raising her hand*): Nothing but the truth, so help me God.

S.C.: That Sunday morning you saw him in church.

ANNA-MARIA: Yes, your Lordship.

S.C.: And you knew it was him?

ANNA-MARIA: Yes, your Lordship.

S.C.: How did you positively identify him?

MALIBU: Does it matter, really?

S.C.: It does, A.C. What if this was a wrong person?

MALIBU: Our defence still stands. The main thing is that she believed he was the right person.

S.C.: Then we must establish beyond any reasonable doubt that she believed he was the right person.

ANNA-MARIA: I know he was the man. I have no doubt about that. He had grown a little bit fat, and more grey. He was much more fat than he used to be.

S.C.: Understandably so.

ANNA-MARIA: But it was him alright. He was wearing an army uniform, very much like yours, which had many medals on it. (*She laughs*) They seemed to be weighing very heavily on him, and he wearily walked towards the altar.

MALIBU: Did you, at that moment, make the decision?

ANNA-MARIA: The medals rattled as he solemnly marched towards the altar, and everyone's attention was on him. He was an august figure, very impressive. (*Laughs*) You know, he was a general. He was in the ruling Military Council. (*Laughs*) I never knew that. I never took any notice who was or was not in the Military Council. Politics is not my line. Who knows, I might have heard his name mentioned on the radio, but never knew he was the man who killed my family.

MALIBU: Did you at that moment make the decision?

ANNA-MARIA: He knelt before the altar, and like the young of a bird opened his mouth to receive the Holy Communion from Father Villa.

MALIBU: Did you at that time make the decision?

ANNA-MARIA: The mouth that was receiving the body of Christ was the same mouth that gave the orders to destroy my family.

MALIBU: For sure this is when you made the decision.

ANNA-MARIA: We are taught to forgive those who have wronged us. I prayed very hard to the Blessed Virgin, to give me strength, and I forgave. Then I saw the man. Although I never really understood the political struggles that led to my family's death, I realised that I never forgave the people who brought it about. The Blessed Virgin never really wanted me to forgive them.

MALIBU (*excitedly*): I told you Prof! I told you! She never forgave them! It is something that lived with her all these years! She never forgave them! This is good, Prof! This is just excellent!

S.C.: You mean, Anna-Maria, it is something that was in your mind all the time, for the last twenty years?

ANNA-MARIA: Oh, no. I never thought about it at all.

MALIBU: But it was there in your mind, although you never consciously thought about it. It was eating you away. You had to do something about it. This is just good, Anna-Maria. You stick to that story and you will be saved.

ANNA-MARIA: It was not there in my mind, and it was not eating me away, and I told you I don't want to be saved. I told you I am not innocent. I told you I want to stay here until my time comes.

S.C.: And what time is that, Anna-Maria?

ANNA-MARIA: Oh, you won't understand.

MALIBU (*softly to S.C.*): It is the time when the Blessed Virgin comes to fetch her, Prof.

S.C.: Poppycock!

MALIBU: It's not for us to judge, Prof. Miracles …

S.C.: … have been known to happen. (*Laughs*) Here on earth the trial continues, and the accused is giving evidence. Then what happened, Anna-Maria? The man opens his mouth to receive the sacrament, and then what happened next?

ANNA-MARIA: The week before my parents were killed there was a lot of political activity in the village. There was talk that the ruling party had lost the election, but was refusing to hand over power to the party that had won.

S.C.: That we know, Anna-Maria. Both of us were active participants in the events of those days.

MALIBU: Do you have to tell her that, Prof.

S.C.: Oh, is it a secret? Are we now going to distort history?

MALIBU: But we must build her confidence in us.

ANNA-MARIA (*ignoring them as they freeze*): Meetings were held everyday at the village meeting square. My father was very active at these meetings. (*Smiles at the memory*) I remember my father wearing his red and blue blanket, riding his brown and white horse to the big rallies that used to be held those days.

She gracefully struts around like a horse.

All the other men of his party would be wearing similar blankets, and would ride their horses in beautiful formations on their way to the rallies. A standard-bearer in a black and gold blanket would lead the formation, reciting poetry that denounced the government and the ruling party, and praised the opposition. Women would ululate and sing in excitement, as the formation passed-by.

She ululates, and excitedly jumps about like a little girl. Throughout all this the lawyers remain frozen.

That is me over there, in a red dress, with big white polka dots. (*Laughs excitedly*) See how we run, on the side of the road, following the trotting horses, and admiring the blankets of the men. Look at my father in his new blanket. We are so proud of our fathers. They are the centre of all the attention of the villagers. And they are our fathers. And here we run on the side of the road admiring our fathers. My father, of course, is much more impressive than other little girls' fathers. The pace of the horses now becomes faster and faster, and we cannot keep up any-more. This time they are going to a distant village where a meeting will be held. So we walk back to our homes.

She ululates again.

That was before the elections. It was during the election campaign. But after the elections things changed at home. There was gloom. Even though my father's party had won there was gloom. I couldn't understand it. When our school wins a netball game or a soccer game, we are happy. We sing and celebrate. And here the adults have won their game, but there is gloom. My mother calls me one night, just when I am getting ready to sleep, "Come with me, child, we have an important job to do." I follow her in the night, and we walk and walk and walk. She is carrying a spade and something in a big paperbag. (*In a little girl's voice*) "Where are we going, mother?" (*In her mother's voice*) "Don't worry, child. You will see when we get there. And do keep quiet. We don't want people to see us. Don't tell a soul about this."

Then we walk and walk and walk. I am afraid of the dark, but when I am with my mother I am not afraid. We get to the outskirts of the village, and my mother starts digging a hole in the ground. She digs and digs and digs. I don't know why she is doing all this. Then she takes out something from the paperbag. It is my father's red and blue blanket. She puts it in the hole she has just dug.

"No! What are you doing, mother?"

"Sh ... People will hear us."

"You can't do this! My father loves that blanket. I love it too."

"We have no choice, child."

"You can't bury my father's blanket!"

"I am burying it to save your father. When they come to search and find the blanket, they will know that father belongs to the opposition party, and they will arrest him."

We walked back to the village in silence, after burying my father's red and blue blanket. Well, not quite silence, for I was snivelling.

She sits down and plays the guitar.

S.C.: What now, A.C.?

MALIBU: Once she does that you can't move her.

S.C.: Is she allowed to do that in the middle of the trial, even before the cross-examination?

MALIBU: She sets her own procedural rules.

S.C. (*desperately*): Anna-Maria, we are still leading evidence. You have to cooperate and answer our questions.

She ignores them, and continues playing.

MALIBU: There is nothing you can do, Prof.

S.C.: What do you mean there is nothing I can do? You do something! Talk to her!

MALIBU: She won't budge, Prof.

S.C.: Anna-Maria, this honourable court wants to know what you did after seeing the General receive the Holy Communion?

She ignores them, and continues to play her guitar.

What went through your mind? At what stage did you
make the decision? Anna-Maria! Anna-Maria!

He stamps his foot on the ground in frustration. Lights fall to black.

SCENE 9

*Lights rise on the Third Space. Anna-Maria is sitting with the four
school girls, playing her guitar and singing. It is much better if this
is not a religious song. It can be any good song that is well-known in
the area so that the audience may participate in a singalong if they
feel like it. It must be a happy song too, for Anna-Maria is in a very
happy mood. Almost at the end of the song Pampiri enters. He stops
and listens. After the song he applauds. The girls kiss Anna-Maria
and scuttle away.*

PAMPIRI: Bravo! A bravura performance!

ANNA-MARIA (*laughing*):   Get out of here. I have been waiting
for you all afternoon. Where were you?

PAMPIRI: Well, I thought Monday afternoons you hold meetings with your Legion of Mary girls.

ANNA-MARIA: Yesterday morning I was in church.

PAMPIRI: So what else is new?

ANNA-MARIA: I saw him. He was going to receive the sacrament.

PAMPIRI (*puzzled*):   You saw him?

ANNA-MARIA: Did you bring your flute?

PAMPIRI: Why, no, I thought you were meeting your girls
this afternoon.

ANNA-MARIA: Well, I am not. I postponed the meeting.

PAMPIRI: I can go and fetch the flute then, if you want us to
play a bit of music. And wait for it, I have a new composition that has been ringing in my head.

ANNA-MARIA: What is it about?

PAMPIRI: Well, I don't know. It has no words.

ANNA-MARIA: Of course silly, it has no words. It is for flute and guitar. But it is about something. Every piece of music is about something.

PAMPIRI: Who did you see in church yesterday?

ANNA-MARIA: Lots of people. The congregation. And Father Villa. He was conducting the service.

PAMPIRI: Well, let me go and fetch the flute then.

ANNA-MARIA: No. Let's rather talk.

PAMPIRI: About what?

ANNA-MARIA (*laughs*): About a man I am going to kill.

PAMPIRI (*laughs*): Okay, let's talk about the man you are going to kill.

ANNA-MARIA: I want you to tell me how to do it.

PAMPIRI: I don't know. I have never killed anyone before.

ANNA-MARIA: But you have imagination, Lawrence. Use your imagination.

PAMPIRI (*laughingly*): I have imagination to create, not to destroy.

ANNA-MARIA: You think you are smart, don't you, Lawrence?

PAMPIRI: If I was smart I would surely understand what you are on about.

ANNA-MARIA (*after a brief pause*): You know, we buried my father's blanket.

PAMPIRI: You told me that story once.

ANNA-MARIA: They came, and didn't find the blanket. They didn't arrest father. They killed him. And mother. And little brother. I never understood why.

PAMPIRI: Usually you don't like to talk about such things. You yourself have always said that they are history, and there is no point of bringing back the past.

ANNA-MARIA: An old nun at the village mission station tried to explain it to me when I was a little girl. But I never really understood it. I thought I did then. It was as though my father was the one who needed my forgiveness for being a communist rather than the people who killed him. Often when such things didn't make sense to me I took refuge in my scriptures. I long forgave my father for being a communist, and through the intercession of the Blessed Virgin I know that God forgave him as well. And yesterday I was looking at the man who killed my family.

PAMPIRI (*hugs her in an attempt to console her*):   Poor child.

ANNA-MARIA (*playfully breaks away from the hug and laughs*): Don't you poor child me. Since when have you turned into a sentimental old fool?

PAMPIRI: Anna-Maria!

ANNA-MARIA: I was talking with the Blessed Virgin last night.

PAMPIRI (*laughs*):   Not again! What is she up to this time?

ANNA-MARIA: I was praying for guidance.

PAMPIRI: What for?

ANNA-MARIA (*jokingly*): As to whether I should kill the General or not.

PAMPIRI: What did she say then?

ANNA-MARIA: She will think about it. I think she will agree with me. She will agree with me that I should kill him.

PAMPIRI: Do you mean a holy personage in heaven would actually agree that you commit murder? As an act of vengeance too at that? Whatever happened to the forgiveness that you people preach about all the time?

ANNA-MARIA: She hasn't agreed yet. But I know she will. Towards the end of the week she will, then on Sunday I'll do it. It is not vengeance, Lawrence. I merely want to clean the world of such filth as the General.

PAMPIRI: Well, if you say so. So how are you going to kill the man?

ANNA-MARIA: I thought perhaps you might advise me on that, Lawrence. On how best it can be done. You are a man of the world, Lawrence. You have read books. You have seen films.

Obviously to Pampiri this is just a big joke. He plays along to humour Anna-Maria, who also treats the matter very lightly, and laughs about it.

PAMPIRI: Maybe you could use poison. Put it in his food.

ANNA-MARIA: I have no access to his food.

PAMPIRI: You told me you are the one who prepares the wine and bread that is drunk and eaten at the communion service.

ANNA-MARIA: You don't eat it, silly. The flakes just melt in your mouth.

PAMPIRI: Whatever. So you can poison one or two pieces of the body of Christ. The pieces that will be eaten by the General.

ANNA-MARIA: That is a very stupid plan. How will I know which pieces will be given to the General?

PAMPIRI: That's a difficult one. Why don't you just take a gun and shoot the bastard and forget about the whole matter.

ANNA-MARIA: You are not being helpful, Lawrence.

PAMPIRI: Well, I don't have any creative ideas on this matter, for crying out loud.

ANNA-MARIA: Where would I get the gun?

PAMPIRI: What's all this ghoulish talk, Anna-Maria?

ANNA-MARIA: I have no way of getting a gun, Lawrence. I wouldn't even know how to use it.

PAMPIRI (*getting impatient with all this useless talk*): Just point it at the General and pull the trigger, that's all.

ANNA-MARIA: You don't have a gun, do you?

PAMPIRI: I would not dream of owning one. What would I do with a gun?

ANNA-MARIA: I don't know. What do people do with their guns?

PAMPIRI: I will tell you what, I have seen one of the priests shoot doves at the Cathedral. You could borrow his gun.

ANNA-MARIA: That's a pellet gun, silly. It wouldn't kill the General.

PAMPIRI: He would feel the pain though.

ANNA-MARIA: And I wouldn't know how to conceal it. It's a long rifle.

PAMPIRI: Oh, you have to conceal it too?

ANNA-MARIA (*laughing*): Be serious, Lawrence.

PAMPIRI: You can get the dove-shooting priest to help you in this mission. If he can kill innocent doves he can kill a guilty General just as well.

ANNA-MARIA: This is my mission, Lawrence. I have to do it myself.

PAMPIRI: I am sure Father Villa has a gun. Why don't you ask him?

ANNA-MARIA: I will find out from the sister who cleans his room.

PAMPIRI: Problem solved at last.

ANNA-MARIA: Not much thanks to you. You have not been very helpful.

PAMPIRI: Who told you about Father Villa's gun then?

ANNA-MARIA: Well, I must go now.

PAMPIRI: I won't see you at all this week. Going for a geography workshop at the university.

ANNA-MARIA: I will see you next week then.

She walks back to the First Space.

PAMPIRI (*calling after her*):   And do try to be merciful, Anna-Maria. Don't kill the poor bastard too painfully. Let's not have too much of a bloody mess.

They both laugh. She sits on her bench on the First Space, and plays her guitar. Pampiri exits, but lights remain on his space. After a few moments Pampiri returns to the Third Space, with his flute. He joins Anna-Maria's music, and together they play, albeit from different spaces. During this piece of music lights rise on the Second Space, and the two lawyers enter, holding their briefcases. After some time Pampiri stops playing, but Anna-Maria softly continues right up to the end of this scene. A peaceful smile rests on her face.

PAMPIRI: Who would have believed she would do it? She stole the gun from Father Villa's room. The next Sunday the General solemnly stands up and walks to the altar to receive the body of Christ. Anna-Maria follows him to the altar. She looks at him and smiles. He congenially smiles back. She takes out the gun and shoots him. There is great commotion. The General dies on the spot. Anna-Maria triumphantly hands herself to the police when they arrive a few minutes later.

S.C.:   This truly is the stuff that melodramas are made!

MALIBU: Premeditated murder is a capital offence. She'd better cooperate.

S.C. (*breathlessly addressing the audience*): My God! A murder in the Cathedral! You can't get more romantic than that.

Lights fall to black on all three spaces. The last strains of Anna-Maria's guitar can be heard in the dark.

SCENE 10

Lights rise on the three spaces. Pampiri stands on the Third Space, Anna-Maria on her bench on the First Space, and the two lawyers on the Second Space.

ANNA-MARIA (*raising her hand*): Nothing but the truth, so help me God.

PAMPIRI (*also raising his hand*): Nothing but the truth, so help me God.

S.C. (*to Malibu*): I see you are still bent on your obsession defence.

MALIBU: Obsession is a form of insanity. So we both agree on the insanity plea.

S.C.: But you have different approach to it.

MALIBU: My argument is that Anna-Maria's emotional growth stopped at the age of nine when she saw her mother raped and her family killed. Would you not agree with me on that, Anna-Maria? I think it is a good defence.

Anna-Maria laughs at him.

ANNA-MARIA: In other words I am a nine year old moron in a twenty-nine year old body. I think it is a stupid defence, if you ask me.

MALIBU: Nobody is asking you in any case. You are in no position to know the difference.

ANNA-MARIA: That's what some smart-arsed lawyer would think.

PAMPIRI: Anna-Maria!

ANNA-MARIA (*giggles*): That's the kind of language I learnt from you, Lawrence.

S.C.:   Obviously the prosecution disagrees with your defence. She was able to relate to people as an adult. She went through high school and through university, and is now a good teacher of mathematics.

MALIBU: My Lord, I object to that.

S.C.:   Your objection is over-ruled.

MALIBU: The prosecution is twisting my words for its own purposes. I am not talking of Anna-Maria's intellectual growth. I am talking of her emotional growth.

ANNA-MARIA: I should know my emotional growth better than anyone of you here.

S.C.:   Proceed, counsellor for the defence.

MALIBU: Thank you, my Lord. It is at that time that she planned vengeance.

S.C.:   What time do you mean?

MALIBU: When she was nine. When her family was raped and killed.

ANNA-MARIA: I have never heard such rubbish in my life; have you Lawrence?

PAMPIRI: They are trying to save you, Anna-Maria.

ANNA-MARIA: They need to save themselves first, before they can be in a position to save anybody else.

MALIBU: My Lord, I will request that I be allowed to lead the evidence without further interference from the accused.

ANNA-MARIA: Accused my foot! Who is the accused here? You or me?

MALIBU: Of course you are the accused.

ANNA-MARIA: If I am the accused then I will talk anytime I want to.

S.C.:   Proceed, counsellor for the defence.

ANNA-MARIA: Okay, I want to change sides. I want to be a witness for the state.

S.C.:   But you are the accused.

ANNA-MARIA: It doesn't mean a thing. I can be state witness as well, can't I. That will save us a lot of time.

MALIBU (*frustrated*): All she wants to do is to mess up our case. She wants to mess up a defence that is destined to live in law reports as a brilliant precedent. A defence that will be cited by scholars, students and great legal minds. She wants to snatch my fame and glory just when ...

S.C.: Please, counsellor! Control yourself. Your defence is not even original. I have come across it in a fictive world. Proceed!

MALIBU: She planned vengeance when she was nine, and was obsessed with it ever since. A nine year old girl cannot be charged with premeditation in any criminal offence.

S.C.: What evidence do you have that her emotional growth stopped at nine?

MALIBU: We have heard from various witnesses already, that often she frolics with schoolgirls, and enjoys playing their silly games. She has never really grown up. She is still a nine year old girl.

ANNA-MARIA: Should I seriously stand here and listen to all these insults directed at my person?

S.C.: You have no choice, Anna-Maria. You are on trial.

MALIBU: My Lord, there has been further evidence that was heard in this honourable court, that when she was at high school, she was heard by the witness who gave evidence here uttering some wish of one day getting even with those who were the cause of her perpetual grief.

ANNA-MARIA: I don't even know the woman who gave that evidence.

S.C.: She was the head cook at your boarding school.

ANNA-MARIA: Then she surely can cook some evidence.

MALIBU: The fact that she resists to be defended proves my point, my Lord. The woman is ...

S.C.: Why do you want to complicate things? Why don't you just come with a simple and straightforward insanity defence. Anna-Maria saw the General, and that suddenly brought back memories. From then onwards until she committed the crime she was not in control of her senses.

MALIBU: The prosecution will shoot holes into that one, Prof.

S.C.: Now for the case of the prosecution, my Lord. Premeditated murder, that's what the state says. Anna-Maria saw the General, and a week passed before she killed him. This was not an impulsive act. It was well-planned. She had a whole week to consider and reconsider her actions.

ANNA-MARIA: That's right. I had a whole week. I didn't just stand up and kill the man. I thought deeply about it. I prayed and meditated about it. What do you say to that?

S.C.: The prosecution agrees with you, Anna-Maria. They disagree that from the age of nine there was no emotional growth. She grew up emotionally and intellectually. She even had a love affair with Lawrence Pampiri.

Pampiri hides his eyes in shame. Anna-Maria giggles. She clearly is enjoying Pampiri's discomfiture.

MALIBU: Objection! Objection, my Lord. No evidence has been led to that effect. The prosecution can't just spring surprises at us.

S.C.: You can cross-examine Pampiri. There he is. Let him take the witness stand.

MALIBU: You had a love affair?

PAMPIRI: I don't think you can call it that.

MALIBU: But you were very close.

PAMPIRI: Very close.

MALIBU: What does that prove, my Lord?

S.C.: They played music together.

ANNA-MARIA: So we did. Big deal!

S.C.: One day they even tried to make love.

PAMPIRI: Tried. Only tried.

MALIBU: What happened?

PAMPIRI: Things didn't work out.

At this point Anna-Maria sits down and plays her guitar.

S.C.: Oh, no, you won't get away with it this time. Every time we get to the most interesting parts you want to play your guitar. We have postponed this trial so many times because of that. This time, Anna-Maria, we are going to hear the evidence without you. Proceed with the cross-examination.

MALIBU: You say things didn't work out. Can you explain exactly what you mean?

PAMPIRI: I have always lusted after her.

MALIBU: And what did you do about it?

PAMPIRI: It was an innocent lust, my Lord. Nothing more.

MALIBU: So nothing happened. You merely had lust in your heart.

PAMPIRI: I have had many fantasies about her.

MALIBU: This only happened in his fantasies, my Lord. I move that this evidence be dismissed with the contempt it deserves.

S.C.: You haven't heard half the story.

PAMPIRI: Well, one day we were playing music together in a deserted science lab.

S.C.: Did you usually play in that deserted science lab?

PAMPIRI: No, my Lord.

S.C.: On this particular occasion why did you choose the science lab? Did you have an ulterior motive?

PAMPIRI: I have always had ulterior motives as far as Anna-Maria was concerned.

MALIBU: So you do admit that you chose the deserted science lab because you had an ulterior motive?

PAMPIRI: We always rehearsed in a particular classroom. But unfortunately on that day it was being painted. So we had to find some other rehearsal space. The deserted science lab was the only alternative.

MALIBU: What happened when you were there?

PAMPIRI: We played some music.

MALIBU: So they played some music. What does that prove?

S.C.: What kind of music? He might be talking figuratively, you know?

PAMPIRI: Oh, different types of music. As we always did. Jazz. Light classics. Sacred music too.

S.C.: So he is not talking figuratively.

PAMPIRI: We tried quite a few of our own compositions. Then I was overcome. She later said I was overcome by the devil. I held her and kissed her.

MALIBU: Did she not resist.

PAMPIRI: She kissed me back.

MALIBU: Oh, my God.

PAMPIRI: We kissed for a long time. Then I lifted her flowing robes.

MALIBU: She let you do that?

PAMPIRI: She did not resist, if that's what you mean. She just froze and said, "Please Mother Mary the Virgin, forgive me for what I am about to do." That did it! That turned me off completely. I just couldn't go on with it. I was so ashamed, I begged her to forgive me. She just laughed and we continued to play our music. I tell you, I was never comfortable with her again after that.

MALIBU: My Lord, how does this prove the prosecution's case?

S.C.: That Anna-Maria was a woman with normal adult passions, and not a child of nine.

MALIBU: My Lord, as far as I am concerned, this new evidence just proves my case. Things didn't work out between the two on that day because Anna-Maria is a nine year old girl emotionally. Normal nine year old girls don't make love.

S.C.: The prosecution takes the position that things didn't work out because of her conscience. She was about to break the major vow of chastity.

MALIBU: Where does that leave us now?

S.C.: The case is adjourned until tomorrow.

They all turned — except Anna-Maria, of course, who remains sitting on her bench and playing guitar — in a military fashion, and give their backs to the audience. They bow, and to the rhythm of Anna-Maria's guitar, slowly march and exits. Lights fall to black.

SCENE 11

Lights rise on all three spaces. On the First Space Anna-Maria and her guitar are not there. Only a pile of her clothes — the habit she was wearing — is on the bench. Father Villa is on the Third Space. Pampiri and the two lawyers are on the Second Space.

PAMPIRI: She's gone!

VILLA: We got a report this morning. They came to inform us that she has disappeared into thin air.

S.C.: How do they account for this?

VILLA: They say they don't know. They woke up this morning and Anna-Maria was nowhere to be found.

PAMPIRI: Just like that?

S.C.: I think a commission of enquiry must be held into this disappearance. Gone are the days when we allowed uncivilised norms to continue unabated as long as our interests were protected.

VILLA: We are not going to support such a commission.

PAMPIRI: And why not?

VILLA: That would be questioning the will of God.

S.C.: Oh, come on, Father. A prisoner disappears from her cell in a maximum security prison and you say God willed it that way?

MALIBU (*it dawns on him*): Father Villa, do you mean …?

VILLA: Yes, Mr Malibu. It must have happened exactly as she said it would.

MALIBU: My God! The age of miracles is not past.

PAMPIRI: Nonsense! I think the Senior Counsel is correct when he says a commission of enquiry must be established.

MALIBU: I think we must respect the wishes of the church as expressed by Father Villa.

PAMPIRI: Let's vote on this.

MALIBU: And who are you? You are just a witness in this case.

S.C. (*laughing*):   You seriously think that the Blessed Virgin came in the silence of the night and took Anna-Maria away? Even you A.C.?

MALIBU: The age of miracles is not past, sir.

S.C.:   Don't be stupid. They whisked her away to kill her.

VILLA: Who did?

PAMPIRI: The soldiers, of course.

VILLA: Why would they do that? I mean right now they are looking for her all over the place. They questioned every nun in the convent. They are seriously searching all over for her. They would not be going through all the trouble and expense if they knew where she was. Anyway why would they want to get rid of her?

PAMPIRI: The trial was exposing too much of the past.

S.C.:   That is not far-fetched, you know. It is well-known that the government would very much like to forget the events and excesses of twenty years ago.

PAMPIRI: The trial was opening old wounds by bringing these things to light, and this was not good for the government, especially now that they have gained some measure of respectability in the international community. The trial was an embarrassment to them.

VILLA: The government is not stupid. You say so yourself that they have now gained some international respectability. Would they jeopardize that by killing the prisoner? Especially when they have such a strong case against her?

MALIBU: With all due respect, Father, the state's case against Anna-Maria was not that strong, especially with the brilliant line of defence that I had devised. Of course this is not to say that I disagree with you when you say the government would be stupid to kill her. In fact I have no doubt in my mind that things happened exactly as she said they would.

S.C.:   A.C., we have always worked on the basis of evidence. What evidence do you have that she was whisked away by the Blessed Virgin?

VILLA: God's ways are not the ways of evidence.

MALIBU: The clothes! She left all her clothes in the cell. That means something. You need evidence, that's your evidence.

S.C.:   Did she fly out of the barred windows naked?

PAMPIRI (*laughs*):   Just like a witch. In our folklore witches fly naked, riding on a broom.

VILLA: That is blasphemy. But what else can one expect from you?

MALIBU: All her clothes are left behind. But her guitar is gone. The soldiers would never have thought of such trick. They are not brilliant enough. That's all the evidence you need.

VILLA: She truly was a saint.

The guitar can be heard in the background, as if from a distance. Father Villa and A.C. Malibu kneel and pray.

S.C: Well, I suppose that brings us to the end of our romantic melodrama.

A haunting flute joins the guitar. Lights fall to black.

MEMBER OF SOCIETY

a play by

Makwedini Mtsaka

This play is dedicated to the fond memory of Kholeka Tile, who was fatally attacked on her way from the rehearsals by some unknown assailants.

MEMBER OF SOCIETY was first performed at the Arts Theatre, East London, on 12 August 1994, with the following cast of characters:

Earlby Ngqisha	—	Felisizwe
Toronto Qumana	—	Nduna
Frank Mabindla	—	Half-a-Crown
Sheila Nante	—	Somi
Nomvuyo Nondlazi	—	Honey
Mvuyisi Ncamane	—	Beast
Tsurie Mahashe	—	Beanstalk
Sheshe Jwayi	—	Japie
Misile Bomvana	—	Jojo
Nandipa Bomvana	—	Pepe
Xolani Sibuta	—	Dancer and Luxolo
Nomathamsanqa Baleka	—	Dancer and Youth
Daluxolo Papu	—	Dancer and Youth

Directed by the author for the SMART SET CULTURAL GROUP

MEMBER OF SOCIETY

PART 1

SCENE ONE

STADIUM: *A group of four youths, two boys and two girls, are seen centre-stage as the lights rise. The two males step forward as soon as music plays backstage and launch into a traditional dance, to the clapping and chanting of the girls. As the performance continues for a couple more seconds all the participants seem to enjoy the occasion. Suddenly a middle-aged man dressed in combat attire enters upstage right and raises his hand immediately to stop them.*

MAN: It's Beanstalk here. I'm surprised to see you guys busy doing indlamu instead of practising your war dance.

JOJO: But it's a nice warm-up.

JAPIE: Don't worry we're just trying to prove a point. Someone out there couldn't believe their eyes when they saw us dancing our hearts out like this.

BEANSTALK: What do you mean? Who are you talking about?

JAPIE: I'm referring to that crowd in front of us there, everybody has been blaming us saying nasty things like we're a youth without a future, we're school drop-outs, we're just people with no culture that's why we don't value anything they do for us no matter how good.

BEANSTALK: And so...?

JAPIE: We've just displayed a splendid cultural act, as you saw, and we hope it'll silence our critics. (*Youths repeat the dance*)

JOJO: That's the kind of stuff that many of us need to inject a bit of fun into our boring education system.

PEPE: ... Yes because some of us are artistically inclined, but who cares among those conservative bureaucrats about our inborn talents?

JOJO: All they are interested in is forcing down our throats pornography, like reproduction of species of some trees, fishes... What a lot of nonsense.

FATIMA: I agree with you, Jojo.

JOJO: I want to know more about me and what this body of mine can do to earn me fame and fortune.

JAPIE: You mean apart from making babies? (*Wry smile as he points at his abdomen*)

JOJO: Shut up, Japie.

FATIMA: (*Fired up*) Look at someone like me, Beanstalk. I'm dead scared of a frog. Now how can I be expected to answer an examination question on its breathing movements?

BEANSTALK: Listen you guys. You've called me here to come and shoot at your trouble-makers, I can't solve your academic problems.

FATIMA: Yes, we're giving you a background...

PEPE: (*To audience*) Our main problem is that we find it difficult to fit into the school system as it is at the moment. (*They all switch into role-playing with her as teacher while the rest act as pupils trying to understand a difficult concept*)

BEANSTALK: Then I've come to a wrong meeting because I'm not an education planner, (*looks at himself*) not with these kinds of clothes I'm wearing.

FATIMA: It's actually the mentality that we want changed, leave the content to us...

PEPE: I want to be involved too as a learner, it's only fair.

BEANSTALK: I'm not a politician, comrades, I'm a fighter and that's what I've come to teach you.

JOJO: Japie, you brought this man in so you'd better handle this fighting business of his... (*Drops out of line*)

JAPIE: Are you chickening out now? (*Handles him menacingly*)

JOJO: We never agreed about fighting. Whom do we fight anyway because the country's laws are changing and ... (*shows optimism with excited action*)

PEPE: Then what do you want here? Why did you agree to be

chosen to represent the student body if you have those kinds of ideas?

JOJO: To make sure that this new education include all the things that I want to be taught.

JAPIE: That's the language of negotiation.

JOJO: So, what's wrong with that?

JAPIE: (*Shakes head, impatient*) Kick the old officials out and employ new ones...

PEPE: Improve the condition of our schools for Christ's sake.

FATIMA: Upgrade the curriculum, and then you can negotiate until the cows come home.

PEPE: And don't favour some schools against others.

JAPIE: Now, Jojo, do you see us achieving all those goals without using a little bit of force?

(*Jojo taps his head*)

FATIMA: Our struggle doesn't need your cultured mind, poor Jojo.

BEANSTALK: There are so many cultures my brother, so you can't just miss out on all of them. (*Counts on fingers*) Culture of tolerance, culture of democracy, culture of learning ... and (*threatens*) culture of violence — of which I'm professor.

(*Japie leads resistance song accompanied by a toyi-toyi.*)

JOJO: I can see we're preparing ourselves for a combat now.

JAPIE: Unfortunately yes. As for the creatures called parents who have bullied us from infancy till now, watch it now! (*Wags finger at audience*)

JOJO: (*Defiant*) Let me make no bones about it, I protest against your kind of protest.

PEPE: Exactly what's the issue here, Jojo?

JOJO: The question is whether we should continue to hurt ourselves while we resist the system.

PEPE: Just try to be clear and stop theorizing.

JOJO: Look at us here we end up being losers many times over. We're roaming the streets instead of keeping our places in the classroom so that one day one of us can become a minister of education.

FATIMA: That makes a lot of sense to me.

JAPIE: You, too, Fatima! … Traitor!

FATIMA: Let's face it, ours is the most troubled generation yet whenever a new minister of education is appointed, he must come from the privileged classes. How come?

JOJO: What does he know about the problems at grassroots level?

JAPIE: All in all what do you want to say to us, Jojo, at this critical moment in our lives?

PEPE: This looks like the turning point.

JOJO: I'm proposing that we adopt a new approach altogether.

PEPE: Explain.

JAPIE: Just in case your new approach means talking to them — you know yourself we've held numerous meetings with our teachers …

PEPE: … pleading our case with the school inspectors …

JAPIE: Trying to convince our parents that the situation is critical, and something drastic must be done about it. We're still in a mess after four years of talking, talking, talking.

PEPE: The shortage of teachers, the overcrowded classes…

BEANSTALK: We've got to get rid of those officials immediately. (*Gestures shooting*)

JOJO: I'm prepared to suffer the consequences but I'm opposed to this idea. (*Points at Beanstalk's firearm*)

PEPE: Exactly what's the problem, Jojo?

JOJO: The way we go about it.

FATIMA: Tell them how you would like us to approach it, Jojo

JOJO: Personally I want to be rational about the whole thing.

BEANSTALK: (*Irritated, paces about*) That kind of thinking is getting you into serious trouble.

FATIMA: Like … what can you do, Jojo? (*To others*) Please give him a chance.

JOJO: First of all, the youth of this country need to live in an atmosphere free of violence or any kind of threat to human life.

JAPIE: Go on, I'm listening …

JOJO: Is anyone taking any control measures on firearms which are on the increase among the youth?

BEANSTALK: That's my department, leave firearms alone.

JAPIE: Nonsense, we're going to carry our weapons so long as our leaders carry them.

BEANSTALK: Yes, they must lead by example.

JOJO: As far as I'm concerned the only weapon the youth must carry is the pen.

JAPIE: But, you can't defend your life with a mere pen.

FATIMA: If you come to think of it we've seen much too much blood in our lives.

PEPE: … and very little ink; eh, Professor Fatima? *(Sarcastic)*

JOJO: Now I've made up my mind, I want to stab paper with the sharp end of my pen.

JAPIE: Comrades, the message is loud and clear, Jojo is quitting our struggle.

JOJO: What struggle?

JAPIE: We're here to protest our rights, we deserve a better education system.

PEPE: Not to mention the frustration of getting no job after you've finished your schooling.

JAPIE: We're still in the dark days of Verwoerd…

PEPE: "It's no use taking the Bantu child to pastures where he'll never graze …"

JAPIE: That's exactly what he said.

JOJO: Those are facts.

PEPE: So what's your case?

JOJO: What role are we playing in harming our cause?

JAPIE: What do you mean? They are the people who're destroying us and ours is to defend ourselves.

JOJO: My friends, it's a big mistake to call them people.

JAPIE: Yes you're so very right. *(Turns to look at the audience)* Animals.

PEPE: … Beasts without a heart.

JOJO: Sorry I didn't mean for you to insult them.

PEPE: It makes no difference …

JOJO: Rather call them ancestors.

FATIMA: What is clear is that every single one of them out there is vengeful against the past.

PEPE: They're armed and shooting in the dark …

JAPIE: And the unprotected youths are their easy targets.

PEPE: That's the point.

JOJO: Who's pulling the trigger, at least now, forgetting about the past?

FATIMA: Now the time has come for us to stop blaming the old apartheid regime. What can we do for ourselves now?

(*Pepe gestures to her to keep quiet*)

JAPIE: Be careful now, Jojo, you're taking your luck a bit too far. Whatever you say don't accuse us of suicide. (*A song is heard offstage*)

Do yourself a favour and disappear quickly. Beanstalk is very cross with you; that's him and his comrades coming. (*Jojo exits*)

FATIMA: It'll be very dangerous of us to dump Jojo just like that. We need him, and let's try and think critically about our situation now.

PEPE: Intellectualising again Fatima…

FATIMA: At this stage of our struggle we are forced to make good decisions about our futures.

JAPIE: But I reject the insult that we're pulling the trigger on us.

FATIMA: You got him wrong, he didn't mean that.

(*Enter Beanstalk*)

BEANSTALK: Where's that sell-out? I'm ready for him now.

PEPE: He's gone.

BEANSTALK: And what about you? The chaps are here to train you.

JAPIE: For the time being Beanstalk we'd like to suspend the armed struggle.

BEANSTALK: Cowards.

JAPIE: We want first to investigate what provisions are made for the young generation in these new welfare laws of theirs.

BEANSTALK: In other words you're ditching me now.

PEPE: No, stick around. All is not final yet.

JAPIE: As a matter of fact we're going to have a meeting with our enemies so we'd like you to skulk around the premises just in case we have need for you.

BEANSTALK: Comrades, that Jojo of yours is a bastard. We must get rid of him. (*He bullies them into submission*)

(*They sing and toyi-toyi as they leave.*)

SCENE TWO

Honey, Nduna, Beast, Somi and Jojo enter with a sense of purpose and act as if they are expecting to meet with someone inside this classroom with broken window-panes. They keep themselves warm by limbering up.

SOMI: I've got an idea. Can't we spend this time of waiting for these children praying? (*Kneels*)

BEAST: (*Impatient*) What for?

SOMI: We want to ask God to bless this meeting with our children.

BEAST: Aren't we blessed to keep the time, arrive here first and wait for them? (*Ridicules her idea by gesturing a prayer to God and utter his speech ceremoniously like a priest*)

SOMI: What can we do? They're our children?

BEAST: Instead I must ask Satan to curse them for showing disrespect to their parents. (*As Somi prepares to put both knees on the floor Honey ministratively rushes across to lay her own scarf so that Somi kneels on it*)

(*Honey leads a prayer song, and is followed by others, except for Beast.*)

BEAST: Now it's my turn to ask their father Lucifer to condemn them to hell. (*Sings pagan song*)

NDUNA: Jojo what time did your friends say they would be here?

JOJO: (*Looks at wristwatch*) They were supposed to be here 45 minutes ago.

NDUNA: (*Looks at own watch*) Little devils. This messes up my day.

HONEY: Never mind. Let's wait, there's all the time in the world.

NDUNA: What's the agenda for the meeting, Jojo?

JOJO: They've theirs, I have mine.

NDUNA: Good boy! Let's start with yours.

JOJO: It's very simple...

BEAST: I like you for that. Damn those villains!

JOJO: Now that everybody is equal, there's no difference between parent and child; teacher and pupil; master and servant, we're all one and the same thing. (*Everybody is shocked*)

NDUNA: Are you crazy? No wonder your friends wanted to kill you.

BEAST: Go to hell. It's impossible that all of a sudden now we're a nation whose children must have no respect for their adults.

HONEY: Please give him a chance to explain what he means.

NDUNA: Go on, Jojo, address the nation and make a fool of yourself.

JOJO: I'm serious ... The new society is just about to dawn on the horizon and so it's going to be a new experience for all of us. And I'm confident the youth are going to take over and run this land.

BEAST: What about our own experiences as old people, which we have gathered over many years?

NDUNA: Besides, your generation is not educated. Don't you think as your parents we have a headstart over you? (*Impatient*)

JOJO: That's what you think, old man.

SOMI: Whatever you do Jojo remember that we supported

and looked after you from birth until now?

BEAST: My boy, is it something like being a born-again Christian?

JOJO: You are not far out but this time religion should not be hijacked by politics.

BEAST: She (*to Somi*) is a very religious person. This one (*to Nduna*) has a philosophical mind so this whole new thing affects them more than us two. (*Gestures to Honey*)

NDUNA: Anyway, I'm not surprised at what this young man says because it was bound to happen like that sooner or later ... I mean those are the natural laws.

HONEY: Nduna, you seem to understand him better. Won't you explain to me what he said.

NDUNA: This is very simple, Honey ... the bottom line is, somehow something is going to change.

BEAST: Then I don't want this change if it's going to happen like what Jojo was saying.

SOMI: I want you two (*Nduna and Jojo*) to answer this question. Is there still going to be God in this new life of yours?

NDUNA: If he's not there, justice will be there.

HONEY: Who's that one?

JOJO: There's no room for newcomers, now.

NDUNA: Go and get Felisizwe. People are very tense here. I've never heard of a leader who stays away from his people at a time of crisis like this. (*To Beast*).

BEAST: All this is the work of that troublesome man called Felisizwe. It was his idea that things should change but look at the shit we're getting from our children as a result. (*Walks towards exit*)

HONEY: Be careful not to be disrespectful; ask him nicely to come. He's a big man now.

SOMI: What do you want us to do, Jojo, now that our lives are going to change?

JOJO: Well, it is important that you accept the new order otherwise you'll be shocked out of your wits.

NDUNA: But it's going to be change at what cost?

HONEY: I hope for the better.

JOJO: All I know is that our values are going to be affected so that we become a new nation. Viva the youth! (*Exits*)

(*Fatima leads song from backstage "Bebehlelele nina.*)

HONEY: Of course there was so much that was wrong in this nation of ours, bloodletting on a big scale and dehumanization of man by man.

NDUNA (*Pats her shoulder*): Don't you worry Honey things are going to be all right.

(*Enter Half-a-Crown dressed in Safari Suit looking very much like an African Leader. Dancers celebrate visitor's entrance*)

ALL: Half-a-Crown ... You are welcome.

NDUNA: What a visit! You mean you've come all the way from Zimlawi?

CROWN: Yes, I've come to wish you all the best for the changes which are taking place in your country.

NDUNA: Who better to wish us well because you went through the same experiences we've had here.

CROWN: I know. Don't bother to tell me brother, but I'm filled with joy to be here now.

NDUNA: My two friends here, Honey and Somi (*Crown shakes hands with them*) can't get over it yet, it all feels like a nightmare to them.

CROWN: Yet it's a reality and they'll soon get used to it.

NDUNA: Myself I'd like to know something, how did the people in your country respond to something like this ... when it came their way?

SOMI: That's a good question, because the news we are receiving about your country is rather mixed...

CROWN: Very much so. There are some pleasing stories but at the same time there are some problems.

HONEY: But I'm sure so long as there are leaders like you there you'll get it right ultimately.

CROWN: Yes, we have only one culture there in my country (*leads Shona song*) ... I'll teach you. It goes something like this ... "

(*Dancers and company transform the scene into a typical African performance in honour of a VIP*)

(*Re-enters Beast*)

BEAST: Felisizwe is on his way here ... I greet you Half-a-Crown, the boss knows you have arrived, he'll be along just now. (*Enter Japie, Pepe, Fatima and Beanstalk singing defiance song*)

BEAST: You're welcome we've been waiting for you all these five hours.

JAPIE: We're not sorry we're late. I'm glad you've come, Half-a-Crown. We've got a couple of questions for you.

CROWN: Fire away my friends.

JAPIE: How did you deal with the youth in your country who did not want to go to school?

FATIMA: We know that their complaints may have been different from ours because your education is not the same as here.

CROWN: What we told them was that Half a Loaf is better than nothing.

BEAN: Half a Loaf of what colour bread? Brown or white?

CROWN: Any thoughts about colour were discouraged in my country if people must become a new nation.

BEANSTALK: Come on old man bread must have a colour. White bread constipates especially if there's no butter on it, brown is recommended for better digestion.

CROWN: Our children didn't ask us those kinds of questions.

PEPE: Anyway what message are you bringing us from Africa?

SOMI: That's a relevant question to ask.

CROWN: This is very important. Regain your humanism-UBUNTU.

PEPE: How does that work?

FATIMA: Yes, what must we do?

CROWN: You've got to work towards interdependence among yourselves. Society is like a chain where every link connects two other parts. (*He makes all of them hook arms together to show strength*) Remember, "I am because we are." Isn't that how the old African saying goes?

HONEY: It also means goodwill towards other people.

SOMI: Respect for your elders.

FATIMA: You're the last people to demand respect from us.

SOMI: Why you pick on us when the devil is in control of your minds?

Black out.

SCENE THREE

Crown is seated on a chair stage-left under a spotlight, with the youths surrounding him

JAPIE: What's your exact mission in this part of the world, Mr Half-a-Crown?

CROWN: I'm moved by the possibility of peace and quiet that could prevail in your region because you know the kinds of problems Africa has gone through before.

JAPIE: But are you now shocked to see this confrontation with our parents?

CROWN: Beyond words.

JAPIE: Mr Half-a-Crown, the only reservation we have about our elder folk is their history. Some of them have proved to be great leaders who selflessly laid down their lives for their countrymen. But there are those who have shamed us when they became homeland leaders.

PEPE: As if that was not enough they pointed the gun at their own people and shot them down whenever they resisted their brutal laws.

CROWN: Oh, let's forget that. It's all history now.

FATIMA: Even the present is not ideal — not when every second government official drives in a Mercedes Benz amid this kind of poverty. (*Gestures around him*)

BEANSTALK: Can I trust a man who called his brothers who were freedom fighters terrorists? Never.

JAPIE: What of their masters whose laws made our lives a

hell on this earth of our ancestors because we did not have that Satan's document called a "pass".

CROWN: (*Frustrated*) By all means remember your past, but work for the future.

FATIMA: Need I say more. In short their laws denied me humanity.

PEPE: Now, don't you think your ubuntu is a non-starter?

CROWN: No. Forgive one, forgive all, my children.

SCENE FOUR

Graveyard is shown by crosses placed in front of the four figures lying on the stage, while Felisizwe is carrying a wreath in one hand.

JAPIE: Before we can be overjoyed about this change it's essential that at least we know what happened to our relatives who were taken away by the Security Police and never returned home.

FELISIZWE: Apparently your sister's grave....

JAPIE: No she never had a grave of her own. There were about five of them all heaped in one shallow hole.

BEAST: For all we know these Security chaps might have come back at night, dug up the bodies, took them away in their vans and God knows what they did with them.

FELISIZWE: I don't understand how people can do that to their fellow human beings.

HONEY: They did that so that there could be no trace of what happened to their victims.

FELISIZWE: Were there no people watching them?

BEAST: They would first make sure that they chased away everyone in the vicinity.

FELISIZWE: There isn't much we can do about the missing graves, but at least we've found your husband's, Honey, and placed a wreath on it.

BEAST: On my brother's grave too, thank you Felisizwe for that.

FELISIZWE: I regard them as our fallen heroes and they'll

always occupy a special place in the annals of our struggle.

JAPIE: I cannot rest until I've found my sister's body.

BEAST: Japie, why don't you let sleeping dogs lie.

JAPIE: She was a human being, Beast, and she was liked by us all in our family.

HONEY: That doesn't mean that Beast is hated by his relatives.

FELISIZWE: How do you feel about all this now, Japie?

JAPIE: I have a lump in my throat.

FELISIZWE: What do you mean?

BEAST: He's finding it difficult to forgive.

JAPIE: How can I forgive when I do not know what they did with her body.

FELISIZWE: What actually happened, Japie?

JAPIE: Three chaps came to our house one early evening. They didn't even knock but gunned for Nzwaki, my sister. They grabbed her by her arms, one on each side while the third one rushed forward to open the car.

FELISIZWE: Did they say what was wrong?

JAPIE: No there was no time to ask them because we were all shocked and that was the last we saw of her.

FELISIZWE: I hear you.

HONEY: It's an experience that no family can easily forget.

FELISIZWE: But you, Honey and Beast, should consider yourselves lucky.

HONEY: I want to confess, Felisizwe, that I'm not hundred percent sure whether that is my husband's grave.

FELISIZWE: You mean where I just laid the wreath?

HONEY: Yes.

FELISIZWE: Why do you doubt?

HONEY: We told you people were always kept a good distance away whenever the police buried their victims.

FELISIZWE: But what makes you feel that one could be where your husband is lying?

HONEY: After three years of guessing which one it might be I decided one day that he's got to have a grave here because this is where their dead bodies were brought and dumped.

FELISIZWE: Does that one have any special appeal to your heart?

(*Honey hesitates*)

BEAST: I just cannot understand women because, Honey, you're the ones who always remark, "Men are all the same."

HONEY: Yes, when we're upset by you but *now* it's different.

JAPIE: Felisizwe, I want you to be very honest with us now. How would you behave if you were in our situation?

FELISIZWE: What is it that'll take you to forgive?

HONEY: Truth.

JAPIE: Someone must tell what they did with their bodies.

FELISIZWE: Would you say generally that's how people feel at the present moment?

ALL: Yes.

FELISIZWE: We shouldn't allow ourselves to be oppressed by a new regime called resentment.

HONEY: All we're asking is give us the real facts then we'll accept the fact that there is nothing we can do about it.

JAPIE: It irritates to be told lies.

FELISIZWE: I thank you for your composure. (*Lights out on Felisizwe washing his hands in a pail.*)

SCENE 5

A hard knock is heard from backstage and after Felisizwe's voice has called out Nduna bursts in looking disturbed.

NDUNA: Felisizwe, fresh fighting has broken out between the taxi rival groups (*Pause*). Can I smoke? (*Takes out a cigarette*)

FELISIZWE: Nduna, by all means be my guest. (*Gestures him to a chair*)

NDUNA: We certainly cannot afford the luxury of armchairs while people are dying in the streets.

FELISIZWE: Just as well you came, Nduna. I meant to warn you not to undermine my achievements.

NDUNA: Far from that. What makes you say so?

FELISIZWE: I heard you're telling people that my appointment is purely the work of some other factors ... It has nothing to do with my own ability as a person. Is that true or not?

NDUNA: Felisizwe, I'm a great believer that sometime or another dynamic forces of history take over and change the pattern of our lives for us, forcing choices on us.

FELISIZWE: (*Impatient*) Make yourself clear.

NDUNA: Of course the little me, you, him and her of this world have put something in that history and there's no denying that fact, but...

FELISIZWE: You talk as if we leaders have no power to influence history with our own intellect.

NDUNA: You know someone once said, "there's nothing so powerful as an idea whose time has come..." Yes, time may have come, but true leaders are not born yet.

FELISIZWE: Who created time, Nduna? We did the moment we said enough is enough from now on we're going to champion the cause of freedom for our people.

NDUNA: Back to the point. What are you doing to stop this shameful incident.

FELISIZWE: Your solution is as good as mine.

NDUMA: You can't afford to take the plight of those so-called ordinary people lightly, you're here because of them.

FELISIZWE: That's the cheapest politicking I've ever heard in my entire life.

NDUNA: I say all this lest we forget and concentrate on our own personal glories at the expense of the people. We must always remember that everyone out there has made a contribution and we've all sacrificed with our lives — Think of those detentions, long jail terms ... what about the stay-aways, the suffering caused by unemployment and no housing, the children's frustrations in and out of school. (*Felisizwe remains speechless except to gesture with his hand in the air*) Granted I'm talking to a man who has suffered it all.

FELISIZWE: Come up with a solution then.

NDUNA: There is only one person who can bring order to this chaos …

FELISIZWE: Why don't you bring him to me immediately?

NDUNA: You're speaking to him at this very moment.

FELISIZWE: (*Pause*) You…?

NDUNA: Yes, me.

FELISIZWE: I've never heard your name mentioned at the people's rallies – at least here in the Eastern Cape.

NDUNA: Yes, I've never gone to any of your rallies — why, because I'm not a member of any political organisation.

FELISIZWE: Well … I don't know what to say.

NDUNA: So you believe in political appointments?

FELISIZWE: Just tell me now, Nduna, what do you want to achieve from all this confrontation with me?

NDUNA: I want to stamp out this curse of violence.

FELISIZWE: You're making a mountain out of a molehill.

NDUNA: Felisizwe, what we're seeing is only a symptom of a deep-seated problem.

FELISIZWE: That's a lie. It's the taxi people who need to organise themselves better. (*Lights go out on them.*)

(*Jojo leads the youth on to the stage, all horrified at the sight of human bodies brought on stage, covered with blood.*)

PEPE: (*Pointing at bodies*) This is the story of thousands and thousands of our people.

JOJO: … with their own hands my people hacked one another and tore their victims literally limb from limb.

PEPE: … allowing themselves to be used as pawns in this power play.

FATIMA: … the perpetrators of these deeds got away with murder and are still at large. If that gets you wondering as to why it is so …

JAPIE: … the long arm of the law is very short in the black communities.

JOJO: ... but then, all this mindless killing ... for what purpose? You may ask.

JAPIE: I do not understand it myself.

FATIMA: ... some evil people out there want us to become disgraced in the eyes of the world.

JAPIE: (*Dismissive*) Third force or not, this must stop.

PEPE: I wish the powers that be could understand that every human life is precious.

FATIMA: ... Before it's too late.

JOJO: I can only hope that this new order will take responsibility over this problem.

JAPIE: ... And not just talk, but do something about it.

FELISIZWE's VOICE: I swear, I shall reconstruct the lives of my people.

SCENE SIX

When lights come up Felisizwe and Nduna are seen together talking in the former's lounge

FELISIZWE: Our people are finding it hard to make a new start in life without thinking about their past experience. I wonder why?

NDUNA: Personally I understand them perfectly well.

FELISIZWE: I know their sufferings, but I'm asking them to grow above them.

NDUNA: Felisizwe, you've asked people to overcome the odds against them and live like normal human beings.

FELISIZWE: Yes. My premise is that it is possible to wipe the slate clean and start afresh.

NDUNA: You reckon?

FELISIZWE: Yes. (*Pause*) It's difficult to make progress in life if you have something hanging at the back of your mind.

NDUNA: When it's been fixed by painful emotions it's not going to be easy to get rid of. I can tell you that.

FELISIZWE: What are you trying to say, Nduna?

NDUNA: I'm trying to say the struggle continues because there are going to be lots of things to moan about still.

FELISIZWE: We shall not be a crying people, there's so much to look forward to.

NDUNA: Fine. But you can't stop us from being a toyi-toying people. (*Enter Japie, Pepe, Fatima and Jojo*)

FELISIZWE: (*Rises from chair*) Believe it or not, the whole country depends on you for its future prosperity.

JAPIE: And you, what's your role?

FELISIZWE: We'll initiate you into this new world.

FATIMA: Perhaps we can't do it all alone. We need a midwife so to speak, to help deliver.

FELISIZWE: I see what you mean.

PEPE: Personally I have a different view to that, Fatima.

FATIMA: Yes ...?

PEPE: We need no one to talk down to us, it doesn't matter who they are.

NDUNA: You don't respect proven wisdom, eh?

PEPE: It's not good to be promised anything if it's not going to be fulfilled.

FELISIZWE: Does that imply that I'm incapable of ...?

ALL: No-o.

FELISIZWE: What is it supposed to mean then?

NDUNA: It goes back to what I said.

FELISIZWE: Hold it, I want *them* to answer.

JAPIE: You keep telling people that they can make a success of their lives while they live in shacks, with no decent roofs over their heads.

FELISIZWE: It's my duty as a leader to instil a sense of purpose in my people.

JOJO: It's grand but it can never fill up my hungry stomach.

NDUNA: I get the message.

FELISIZWE: Bring your leadership to me, I want to give them good advice.

JOJO: We'd rather have this foreigner, Half-a-Crown, do that.

FATIMA: That's what I meant by a midwife.

ALL: Yes, that's the people's choice.

(*Blackout*)

SCENE SEVEN

When the lights come on again enter Crown guiding a young man who's all bare except for a napkin around his bottom. He staggers like a baby learning to walk, and this action takes a rhythmic form as the music backstage becomes dance like, then he launches into a full-blooded dance. All the actors watch and cheer him on by clapping hands and stamping their feet with joy. Then they all grab hold of the youngster and raise him high as Crown pronounces his names. Musicians' instruments play as each name is called out.

CROWN: Today we name you Rholihlahla, Mangaliso, Albert, Bantu...

SOMI: Lilian ...

HONEY: Helen ...

CROWN: Of course, what's in a name after all?

ALL: (*Shout*) Luxolo. (*Music and excitement*)

CROWN: That's a name by which you will be known to the world at large, Luxolo.

SOMI: Luxolo, so that there can be peace in our land.

(*All actors come forward to offer him a present each, then again they mime a dove which they all liberate at the same time while starting to sing and dance.*):

> "Fly away white dove
> Fly away
> You are our messenger
> Of peace to the country at large
> Peace to the continent
> Peace to the world.
>
> May the names of our heroes
> Which we have bestowed

Upon you act
As a symbol of hope
Self-sacrifice and love
Of mankind

Soar up high in the sky
White dove
Go tell the Almighty
That we're free at last
Don't forget to tell him
That we need his blessings
Fly away white bird of peace.

CROWN: This child signifies the long journey we all must undertake before we can arrive where we want to get to.

FELISIZWE: Luxolo, welcome to the world and make it your world.

FATIMA: What is in it for him?

FELISIZWE: He must become humane, and take his rightful place amongst other citizens of the world.

NDUNA: Crown, I find all this puzzling. What does it really mean in terms of our specific needs here?

CROWN: Reconstruct yourselves so that you can become a new nation.

BEAST: I fear the responsibilities that come with that.

CROWN: You must have a positive image of yourselves.

NDUNA: Felisizwe, you have to lead by example, Luxolo has shown us.

He strips Felisizwe of his clothes except for the undertrousers. Everybody looks stunned. Black out

PART 2

SCENE ONE

Felisizwe and a group of youths are celebrating with song and dance. A knock is heard after which Crown enters.

FELISIZWE: Crown, I'm pinning all my faith on you.

CROWN: Not when I have to go back home as soon as possible. I only came here to rejoice with you.

FELISIZWE: I need a mirror (*Crown positions himself as one*) to reflect what I do.

CROWN: I'd say first to reflect who and what you are.

FELISIZWE: Is that any different from what I said?

CROWN: Very different my brother, you must first assume a new identity so that you do what you do because of who you are. (*Gives him whisk and places hat on his head.*)

FELISIZWE: Well put…

CROWN: Well dressed. (*Admires him.*)

FELISIZWE: But can't the world see from what I'm wearing that I'm a new person now?

CROWN: We're here to confirm your identity, it's not good enough for you to wear your short pants. We all have ours in our wardrobes and we can put them on any summers day.

FELISIZWE: You are just being difficult for nothing.

CROWN: The standards are high my brother, you've got to live up to them.

FELISIZWE: I do not deny that, but I need more than this. (*Gestures at flywhisk and woollen hat.*)

CROWN: The moment your vision is in agreement with what you wear…

FELISIZWE: (*Stops him with gesture*) So much for your idea of identity.

CROWN: Are we speaking the same language or not, Felisizwe?

FELISIZWE: I must tell you that you have your own English language in the rest of Africa, but what you need to know is that South Africa is a very rich country. We can afford to buy ten times as many text books as you can.

CROWN: Books full of slogans, but no substance for your young people who are hungry for knowledge.

FELISIZWE: The more there are the better.

CROWN: The difference is we read the few we have with understanding.

FELISIZWE: I shall not take any more of that arrogance from you. (*Throws flywhisk and hat to the floor.*)

The youths go out.

CROWN: Be careful Felisizwe, I'm not your subject.

FELISIZWE: I don't care. You came here at my invitation, so you've no right to say just anything you like. (*Paces about stage*) I may be wearing shorts but I'm not a child born yesterday, all I'm doing is trying to demonstrate to the people that we've got to crawl first and then go through all the stages of development before we can become what we want to be.

CROWN: Don't crawl into the fire, or worse still don't become a deviant child.

FELISIZWE: Shut up now Crown I've had enough of your insults. (*Change of lights to dim, then enter Nduna, and Beast.*)

CROWN: It's still too early for you my friend to become angry.

NDUNA: We're concerned because we heard you shouting at each other.

FELISIZWE: Fancy this Half-a-Crown of yours saying I must not become a deviant child. (*Exits*)

BEAST: Did you really say that, Crown?

CROWN: Yes, it was in the spirit of brothers exchanging ideas.

FELISIZWE: Insults! That's the only thing we exchanged.

BEAST: Personally I'm offended on his behalf. Don't you miss your country now, Half-a-Crown? (*Shouts*) Beanstalk, come here quickly. (*Enter Beanstalk*) Escort this man to the airport.

BEANSTALK: (*To Crown after salute*) Beanstalk is at your service.

NDUNA: Just a minute, Beanstalk.

BEAST: Our leader has been insulted, keep this man a minute longer he'll eat Felisizwe raw.

NDUNA: Half-a-Crown do you have any problem with how things are going at the present moment?

CROWN: (*Brightens up*) Why do you ask that question, are

you suspecting that something wrong is happening?

NDUNA: I just want to know if everything is all right.

BEAST: Especially that you were nasty to Felisizwe.

CROWN: The word "right" does not exist in our vocabulary, my brother.

BEAST: I thought so, you use poor dictionaries.

NDUNA: Does that mean then that everything you do is all wrong?

CROWN: We allow no one to sit in judgement over our actions.

BEAST: Then what's all this fuss about; telling our leader how to do things.

CROWN: I didn't tell him to do anything, I only asked him to take on an identity of his own. (*Nduna nods recognition of idea*)

BEAST: Can you follow what he is trying to tell me, Nduna?

NDUNA: What about my own feelings? Never mind what you want to know. Felisizwe must respond to the needs which are felt by the people on the ground and not try to fit the stereotype of a leader who adheres to an ideology which has no use for the masses just because some of his great comrades believe in it.

BEAST: Mhm! I now doubt your loyalty to this great comrade, Nduna.

NDUNA: You surprise me sometimes, Beast.

BEAST: How come you sound so doubtful about him?

NDUNA: Am I not supposed to think as an individual?

BEAST: That was not very patriotic of you to think like that.

NDUNA: I'm entitled to my thoughts, so is everyone of us in this country.

CROWN: Talking about that, how do the people in the, communities feel about their lives now? (*Moves upstage as judge*)

NDUNA: I think they don't understand their own feelings, so they'd rather keep quite, and also they're very cautious about every little step they take.

BEAST: Through no fault of Felisizwe?

NDUNA: It's his duty to make us speak out and say what we

think otherwise too much silence will kill us all.

BEAST: (*Shouts*) Beanstalk, here's one more customer for you. There are two offenders now.

CROWN: It's the responsibility of each and every one of you to talk with each other. (*Addresses the audience too.*)

BEAST: Back to one person, Beanstalk, I like what Crown is saying.

Snap blackout

SCENE TWO

Enter Felisizwe followed by all the youths. Fanfare of trumpet is heard.

FELISIZWE: These young people have been working hard to achieve our goals. (*To youths*) Tell them what you've been up to.

JAPIE: We've been trying our damndest best to get all communities to participate in common programmes.

NDUNA: (*Everyone excited, Crown links their hands together*) Any luck?

JOJO: So far we've been unsuccessful.

FELISIZWE: Let them know how indifferent some of the communities were to you.

FATIMA: What about those who were abusive and said that they don't want to have anything to do with us?

(*Dancers present agitation ending up with "Kubo"!*)

PEPE: They are not keen to lower their high standards.

JOJO: Black communities too are very much agitated.

CROWN: It must be very discouraging to young people like you who are expecting a great deal from this change.

PEPE: I was actually shocked to hear all the things they said about us, and did they insult our Political Party.

NDUNA: That's the price we must be prepared to pay. Was that your experience Half-a-Crown?

CROWN: Much worse than this. The difference is only the tip of the iceberg, my friend.

JAPIE: It's so frustrating I feel like showing my bottom to someone (*Turns upstage as if to strip*)

FELISIZWE: And why isn't this change the best solution to our problems? Who's behind all this conspiracy?

CROWN: Don't worry they want it on their own terms, typical.

FELISIZWE: What do you think lies at the heart of our problems?

CROWN: Felisizwe you may mean well, but is everybody else sharing your ideas?

BEAST: You must just be careful not to force-feed people with liberation otherwise they'll spit it in your face.

(*Felisizwe stares at Beast disapprovingly*)

I mean some people are not fit to take any responsibility, but they're getting paid just for laughing at their colleagues mistakes.

FELISIZWE: Crown, my question still stands, why won't people accept a change for the better?

CROWN: Why don't you change your company?

FELISIZWE: You've made your point.

CROWN: These are the people who are hardest hit. (*Points at the youths*)

FELISIZWE: (*To youths*) Tell Uncle Feli, what do you want me to do for you?

1ST YOUTH: We want to get a ride on the train and simply go away somewhere.

NDUNA: Which one exactly? There are too many trains nowadays.

FELISIZWE: Is that all you want?

2ND YOUTH: We want to be protected so that our lives are safe.

FELISIZWE: Go on tell Uncle everything you want.

3RD YOUTH: I want to be able to save people's lives when I'm grown up.

4TH YOUTH: Personally I want my wife and my children to be safe and free from harm, when I'm an adult.

FELISIZWE: But I haven't heard anyone say that I want a drug-free society. I don't want to taste liquor with my lips,

certainly no one has said I don't want to harm anyone. (*All youths improvise a song and dance performance on drugs, liquor abuse, and violence.*)
Blackout

SCENE THREE

Same place.

CROWN: (*Authoritatively*) The overriding thing is that we all have to see it as a process.

FELISIZWE: Can I hope that other people too are going to see it in that light?

BEAST: Mhm! That's exactly what Africa is all about, changing names all the time so Crown we must stop calling it "liberation", its correct name is "process"?

CROWN: By that I mean, my brother, anything, any activity is a process if it is at the stage of development.

FELISIZWE: You don't have far to look for evidence of that.

CROWN: All of us beyond Limpopo River are engaged in the process of liberation.

NDUNA: Yes, but we must look at South Africa from a different perspective, there are no worse colonised Africans than us here.

BEAST: (*Points at Nduna's clothes*) You are the first one.

CROWN: Didn't I talk about identity to you?

NDUNA: I don't wear safari suits, I'm not a bloody hunter.

CROWN: Felisizwe, it's vital my brother that you people acquire your own identity. (*An excited noise of singing, ululation, chanting of traditional praises is heard off-stage: a crowd of revellers dressed in indigenous costumes escort a young man who is covered with a blanket and on reaching stage-centre he discards it and starts to dance as an umkhwetha to the utter enjoyment of spectators.*)

HONEY: (*Steps forward*) We just hope Half-a-Crown will stop insisting that we obtain ID's because what you just saw,

Sir speaks volumes about who we really are as a people and there is no need to be identified by other people the way they want. (*Crown is mortified by embarrassment from this error*)

NDUNA: (*Embarrassed*) Eeh-in-eeh! He certainly didn't mean an ID book with your nice face on it, he spoke of identity.

HONEY: Oh I see, please forgive me.

CROWN: You're welcome. It's unlike that document which bears an imitation of your face, no one can take away this kind of identity from you because no one gave it to you except your ancestors. (*Admires her traditional garb*).

HONEY: I'm glad then that our customs can be part and parcel of this new identity. (*Then she leads the group into her own traditional song and dance, clapping hands*)

SOMI: What about the kind of education we received in the lap of our grandmothers, when we listened to the fantastic stories they told us. (*Sits on a pillow and gestures the youths to sit in front of her as she takes Pepe by the arm and rests her head on her lap*) My children, your generation has missed out on really good education which came directly from our parents; not your televisions, radios and newspapers.

JOJO: For heavens sake Somi the stories you were told have no relevance to our modern lifestyle. What lessons can I learn from the adventures o the jackal, wolf, tortoise, sea bird, the whole lot?

SOMI: Our elderly folk knew exactly how these stories were supposed to affect our young impressionable minds.

JAPIE: Do you mean you expect us in the twentieth century to believe in animals which spoke a human language?

JOJO: That's not real.

HONEY: That's what you haven't got. A human language … the result is you resort to fighting to make your point.

SOMI: The words those animals speak my boy have shaped and moulded our characters as humans.

JOJO: I refuse to accept that our modern technology must be submitted with intsomi, stories and fables.

FELISIZWE: (*Reassures him*) Okay Jojo there is a place in our new society to use all those ideas and restore people's values.

BEAST: What do you say, Crown?

CROWN: That's the best option; for our continent to be recognized for the role we play in the modern world while we at the same time respect our past.

BEAST: Is that why you walk around carrying that thing (*points at flywhisk*) in your hand?

CROWN: Yes and no.

BEAST: (*Shouts*) Beanstalk, there's a fresh problem for you come quickly. (*Beanstalk enters*) What do you think of this? (*Points at flywhisk*)

BEANSTALK: I know the SPCA will regard this as cruelty to animals.

CROWN: And so?

BEANSTALK: They'll probably see to it that you're arrested for cutting a cow's tail like that.

CROWN: This has no comparison to the hundreds of thousands of livestock they stole form our forefathers. Let us be reminded that once upon a time I had cattle (*Shapes arms like horns wistfully*) But now I've **nothing**.

BEANSTALK: You've been left clutching a cow's tail.

CROWN: If you like.

BEAST: I hope that's not what you want us to appear like in the eyes of the outside world, a dignified African man holding a tail but the meat is taken by someone else.

BEANSTALK: Is that the kind of identity you want for us, Crown?

BEAST: You know when you first arrived I was pretty drunk but now I'm sobering up and I'm smelling a rat.

JAPIE: Crown is that a fair accusation? (*All actors on stage shout out insults as the voices rise to a crescendo that drowns any attempts by Crown to defend himself until blackout saves him from violent attack which looks imminent*).

SCENE FOUR

When lights come up Felisizwe, Nduna, Somi and Honey are seen discussing.

SOMI: Felisizwe, I didn't like the behaviour of the people towards Crown.

FELISIZWE: I agree, It was the most disgraceful thing I've seen.

HONEY: Who caused the whole thing?

SOMI: It was that man called Beast, helped by his friend Beanstalk.

HONEY: He's lived up to his ugly name, hasn't he?

SOMI: What picture does it paint of us?

HONEY: Gorillas, that's what we behave like.

SOMI: Felisizwe, it's clear that Beast is the enemy of the people and I strongly feel that he must be disciplined.

NDUNA: This is a crisis, and we're forced to take a decision.

FELISIZWE: I don't think it's as serious as that.

SOMI: We've got to know what was the motive behind all this.

HONEY: I suggest we must first try and understand the kind of person Beast is then we'll know why he did this.

SOMI: He's a spoiler, but that's not going to help us here.

HONEY: More than that he likes to stand out from the crowd and be noticed.

NDUNA: It'll sound very harsh on my friend Beast but he has inborn contempt for our African leaders on the continent.

FELISIZWE: Besides everything else you're saying about him he was very much disturbed by Crown's unkind remarks against me.

SOMI: There's no place in our society for those individuals who are touchy about criticism.

HONEY: Similarly anyone who acts independently from the rest of other people must be brought to order.

NDUNA: He's been brought up to believe that he's better and more progressive than his brothers and sisters over there.

HONEY: If he had taken Crown's ID business seriously he'd have saved his face.

FELISIZWE: Obviously he found it hard to take Crown's advice that we should be dressed like him.

SOMI: (*Impatient*) What do we do about his behaviour Felisizwe?

FELISIZWE: Do we have to do something about it as if he's committed the worst crime on earth?

SOMI: How else do you deal with an offender who has put our reputation at risk like this?

FELISIZWE: Ignore him and go on with the good work you're doing, and ultimately that's what matters.

NDUNA: Felisizwe with respect, but I must tell you that you've connived at this mischief for reasons best known to you.

FELISIZWE: I deny that.

NDUNA: This whole thing smells of favouritism and I want to be no part of it. (*Exit*)

HONEY: What is going to happen to the morale of the people now, Felisizwe, when tempers flare up like this?

FELISIZWE: I'm nobody's fool, Honey. This rivalry between Nduna and Beast goes back more than thirty years and I'm not going to allow either of them to use me to gain favours over the other.

SOMI: It's becoming all complicated now. But you still have to take a decision against anyone who offends. I don't care who he is.

NDUNA: (*Chuckles*) I know why Beast did that. He thought that I have won Half-a-Crown over to my side so that I can bargain for more power by using this foreigner.

HONEY: Also Nduna's problem with Beast whatever its source seems to be coming to a climax at the wrong time.

SOMI: And for the sake of peace we need to know why Nduna seems very impatient with Beast.

NDUNA: That's a very delicate issue which only Nduna knows about apart from Beast.

SOMI: I beg you to solve this problem for us Felisizwe. (*Takes out a bible*) And I shall ask you to swear on this Bible to maintain the peace here. (*A loud knock is heard from backstage*)

FELISIZWE: (*Shouts*) Who's that? (*Tries to escape*)
(*Enter Beast and Beanstalk followed by Japie, Jojo, Fatima and Pepe. They drive Felisizwe back on to the stage centre.*)

JAPIE: We've made an interesting discovery about these two gentlemen (*Points at Beast and Felisizwe*)

JOJO: Our honourable leader.

PEPE: And our not so honourable comrade Beast…

FATIMA: … Are brothers, born of the same father but different mothers.

SOMI: Is everybody here, Japie?

FELISIZWE: (*Secretly*) That's the secret I've been nursing.

SOMI: It's too late now to sit over it.

BEANSTALK: Someone has spilt the beans already.

NDUNA: I've known all along that these two gentlemen are related and I've had no reason to worry about it, they've a right to be brothers but from our experience having brothers in one administration is a recipe for corruption. (*To audience*) You know what I mean.

HONEY: The question is, if I don't have a brother amongst you…

(*Enter Crown*)

CROWN: This is a hullabaloo about nothing.

HONEY: Do I really belong here?

CROWN: Yes.

JOJO: Half-a-Crown you'd be better advised to stay out of it.

JAPIE: Especially in view of the many accusations of nepotism we've read about your neighbours.

CROWN: Now it's very clear to me that I'm an undesirable element in this country of yours. (*Baggage over his shoulder.*)

FATIMA: Please don't go yet, we're going to have a glorious party for your farewell.

CROWN: I must go now. Good luck Felisizwe for the future success of your country. Salani Kahle.

FATIMA: Not before we know what's going to happen to us.

BEAST: Hamba kabi.

PEPE: Crown, you've not fulfilled your task yet.

NDUNA: Where does this leave us?

FATIMA: I am very much uncertain now.

LUXOLO: When are we becoming members of this new society?

JAPIE: I suppose when we've learnt to stand on our own hind legs.

BEAST: … and be fully grown up like Luxolo.

(Music and dance are performed by the youths to assert themselves by pushing the adults to the sides of the stage while they occupy centre-stage in a symbolic fashion.)

CURTAIN